"*Finding Peace with Your Body: A Body Image Guide for Women* by Johanna Kulp, MSW, LCSW, is a powerful resource for anyone trying to reclaim a better body image! Her book is filled with strategies and client examples that demonstrate the layers of disrupted body image. I especially loved the chapter on trauma, the impact it leaves on one's image and how to create physical and emotional safety to heal one's body image. Readers will gain enormous insight into the role of self-compassion to create change, in the aftermath of a multitude of mental health struggles. I will be recommending this book to trauma survivors, supporters and clinicians who treat warriors of eating disorders, body dysmorphia and trauma!"

Shari Botwin, LCSW, *trauma therapist, author, media contributor and expert witness*

"For anyone who has ever thought their body was not good enough, this book will make you think and be at peace with your body. Writing with an engaging blend of personal narrative, case studies, psychological research and therapeutic advice, Johanna Kulp challenges everything the diet industry and diet culture has wrongly told you for years. You will long reflect on what you learn from this book."

Dr. Margaret L. Andersen, *professor of Sociology Emerita, University of Delaware*

Finding Peace with Your Body

Finding Peace with Your Body weaves together the author's personal story as well as her work as a psychotherapist to create an interactive self-help guidebook to help readers find harmony with their bodies. This is an interactive book with a fresh perspective that encourages the reader to dive deeper into their own personal history and use this book as a place to journal and complete specific homework instructions to change their relationship with their body. This book includes personal anecdotes, theoretical orientation and specific clinical intervention in a way that helps the reader understand context, personal experience and the ability to create direct behavioral and cognitive change in their life. The journey map includes not only reflective prompts but also weaves in historical context regarding the subjugation of women's bodies throughout time. Organized so that it can be used by individuals or practitioners assisting their clients along the journey of recovery from an eating disorder, this book offers readers hope, practical tools and a road map for working through specific body image issues with practical skills and therapeutic interventions.

Johanna Kulp, MSW, LCSW, is founder and owner of Live Well Therapy Associates, a psychotherapy practice in Philadelphia, PA. She has 15+ years' experience helping those in eating disorder recovery.

Finding Peace with Your Body

A Body Image Guide for Women

Johanna Kulp

Routledge
Taylor & Francis Group

NEW YORK AND LONDON

Designed cover image: ©Getty Images

First published 2025
by Routledge
605 Third Avenue, New York, NY 10158

and by Routledge
4 Park Square, Milton Park, Abingdon, Oxon, OX14 4RN

Routledge is an imprint of the Taylor & Francis Group, an informa business

ISBN: 9781032654782 (hbk)
ISBN: 9781032654775 (pbk)
ISBN: 9781032654799 (ebk)

DOI: 10.4324/9781032654799

Typeset in Optima
by codeMantra

To my children—Adelyn, Blaine, & Isaac.
You have brought such joy to my life.
Thank you for all that you are.
Here's to breaking patterns for all future generations.

Contents

Introduction

Picture this. You're in a room with 100 women. There are women from all walks of life and all ethnic and racial backgrounds. There are trans women and cis women. There are women of all ages, from 9 to 90 years old. And get this: 91 of these women have experienced body hatred, body shame or disordered eating patterns at some point during their lives (*11 Facts About Body Image*, n.d.). No one is immune to these issues: not the 9-year-old and not the 90-year-old.

This is staggering data. And if you are picking up this book, I imagine that you may find yourself in a similar state of mind. You're not alone. Two questions loom large: How did we get here? What is the way out? I can guarantee that the way out isn't found in the latest fad diet or a new exercise regimen. If it were, then we wouldn't see nearly 100% of the female population believing that their bodies are not good enough.

I've been in the depths of self-hatred myself, and although the task to find body acceptance is not easy, there is a way out. That's what this book aims to do—to give you the tools, skills and resources that will help you move beyond the endless cycles of body-related self-hatred and diets. This book will act as a bridge between the experiential, the academic and the clinical worlds. In my own personal journey, I found myself needing a guide to help me through what felt like an insurmountable task of finding peace with my body.

With this book, I hope to give understanding of how we got to this place as a society as well as how to find freedom personally. This requires both a societal view and examining individual experience. The connection between the two is incredibly important: Social norms exist not only "outside" of us but also "inside." Freedom can

DOI: 10.4324/9781032654799-1

come in both places, by finding peace individually and advocating shifts in society.

As we journey through this book, I will be discussing my own process, drawing from experiences that I had in both my hardest body image years and my path toward healing. As a psychotherapist who specializes in eating disorder issues, I have heard no shortage of stories and experiences similar to my own body image narrative. To honor the variety of experiences and to help create an increased connection for your healing journey, I will share pieces of my clients' stories and their healing. To protect identities and ensure confidentiality, I'll weave these stories together.

Body Image Affects All of Us

I emphasize that body image issues impact more than one group of people, so we cannot lose ourselves in just one narrative. My perspective is as a white cis woman raised in the 1980s and 1990s, but poor body image occurs at staggering rates across all genders, ages, races and ethnicities. To stick to only a small subset of the population is to miss how negative body images occur across many other diverse populations.

Stories from my clients will include those of varying ages and races as well as those of trans women. We are not just up against an issue that impacts cis-white women. Women from all walks of life are feeling the negative impact from cultural ideals and pressures.

A recent study found that the number of men hospitalized for eating disorder issues increased by 53% from 1999 to 2009 (Eating Disorder Statistics, 2024). Unrealistic body standards are no longer simply a "woman's issue." Although the occurrence of unrealistic ideals is still higher among the female population than among the male population, it is on the rise by more than 50% in cis-male populations. Furthermore, transgender individuals experience eating disorders at a higher rate than cis-gender individuals (Swanson et al., 2011).

Not to get lost in numbers or research, but the important point is that restrictive body images have a severe impact on all people—people of varying genders, ages and ethnicities. We are up against an epidemic of poor body image. As a culture we are not addressing this as we need to.

We are up against an epidemic of poor body image and as a culture we are not addressing this as we need to.

I share small pieces of recovery stories not because I believe that your experiences will match mine or my clients' specifically. My hope is to intertwine parts of my experience as well as my work as a psychotherapist with eating disorders to help you see that the poor body image you are experiencing does not have to last for a lifetime, that others have been in your place and that they have found their way through. You can get to a space of where you know your body is doing just what it is supposed to do too—moving, giving you life and functioning for you.

You are not alone in your feelings about your body. You are not alone in your history. You are not alone now. I've seen many clients reclaim their relationship with their bodies: I have done this. You can as well. Yes, it is possible to find peace with your body.

Yes, it is possible to find peace with your body.

Let's start at the beginning and move forward from there. We'll deconstruct the messages we took in and rebuild together.

How to Use This Book

If you're reading this book, chances are that you are finding yourself stuck in some way with food and body image. I was there. I know the feeling well. I hope to show you a way out. My journey was long and winding and didn't follow a neat and tidy way up. But I got to a place of security with my body and myself, and I believe you can too. It is possible to have a positive relationship with your body. Your path will not look exactly like mine—each of us walks our own path and journey. But I want you to believe in your resiliency to see yourself through.

Together we will deconstruct our beliefs about our body and reconstruct together. It's a rebuilding.

Each chapter focuses on a different part of the body image healing journey. I will first define body image, describe the process of recovery and examine how poor body image thoughts may have developed in your own life. This includes both the societal and familial impacts on our belief systems. Then I discuss the deeper roots of feminine ideal body types throughout time and how the media create (unattainable) body image ideals. I survey diet culture and its impact on our beliefs as well. It's important that we start by looking at this background first; if we don't pay attention to how the thoughts and feelings about our body came to be, we're stuck believing the validity of these thoughts. We need this reality check as ammunition against negative self-talk and thinking.

We then dive deeper into our own mental, emotional and behavioral health and its impact on our body image. In these sections we engage at the personal level of dissecting and evaluating our thoughts, changing our own mind's script and finding a new language to use with ourselves. From this we can change what we experience when we view ourselves in the mirror. The focus is on first changing the script in our minds, helping us work toward acceptance and then kindness, compassion and care for our bodies and ourselves.

At the end of each chapter, I include journal prompts for you to consider. Throughout each chapter, you will find break-out boxes that discuss therapeutic terms and clinical interventions. It is very important to pause and write your thoughts on these topics and ideas. Doing so helps connect what you are reading in this book and your own process.

I reassure you that there is hope and that you can feel secure, free and even content with your body. That hope does not come from the latest popular diet, a number on the scale or the absence of cellulite, which is a normal part of a woman's body! Instead, your change comes from accepting that your body, our bodies and ourselves as humans deserve space in this world. There is nothing wrong with the size of your thighs or shape of your stomach. The wrongness lies in an industry that makes profits from women hating themselves and their bodies. There is a culture born of that industry.

There is nothing wrong with the size of your thighs or shape of your stomach. The wrongness lies in an industry that makes profits from women hating themselves and their bodies. There is a culture born of that industry.

Strap in and let's get started.

References

11 *Facts About Body Image*. (n.d.). DoSomething.org. https://www.dosomething.org/us/facts/11-facts-about-body-image

Eating Disorder Statistics. (2024, March 8). *National Eating Disorders Association*. https://www.nationaleatingdisorders.org/statistics-research-eating-disorders

Swanson, S. A., Crow, S. J., Le Grange, D., Swendsen, J., & Merikangas, K. R. (2011). Prevalence and correlates of eating disorders in adolescents. Results from the national comorbidity survey replication adolescent supplement. *Archives of General Psychiatry, 68*(7):714–723.

Part 1

An Understanding and Background on Body Image

Chapter 1

Defining Body Image

Myth Debunked

"If I just lose another 5. . .10. . .15 lbs, then I'll be happy in my body."

Losing weight will not make you happier in your body. I know that what I just said stands in contrast to everything we hear around us. If we look to changing our body in order to like our body, we are only answering half the story. We are not addressing or healing the years of self-hatred memories or the pain that we've experienced in relation to our bodies.

If changing our body in order to like our body worked, it already would have worked by now. 5 or 10 pounds is a bandaid to the deeper need to heal yourself, care for yourself and learn to have a relationship again with this body that is here and now. We cannot make something better by distrust, self-hatred, negativity and shame. We cannot internalize negativity and expect that a shift in our body size will change that.

We need a new language, a new connectivity and a new way of caring for and relating to our body to do this. Losing weight is not the goal. Care, compassion and connection are the goal.

To shift our own relationship with our body, we need to create a deeper understanding of body image and what it means. Ask yourself:

- What first comes to mind when you think of body image?
- Do you picture chiseled abs or perfect hourglass shapes?

DOI: 10.4324/9781032654799-3

- Do you think of magazines with tips on how to get your beach body ready?
- Do you long for body of someone you admire?
- Is there shame related to how you see your body?

"Too wrinkly, too big, too jiggly." Those are some of the thoughts I've heard from others or had myself in the past.

Let's boil down body image to its most basic definition from *Webster's Dictionary*: Body image is "the *subjective* picture or mental image of one's own body."

The word "*subjective*" is key. A person's self-perception is neither objective nor factual. Body image is a feeling or belief system about yourself. Let's say that again: Body image is how you *feel* about your body. It is not about how you look in reality.

I have had my own personal struggles with poor body image. I've heaped negative and unfair thoughts on my body throughout the years, comparing myself to others.

How is it possible to exist in this society—especially as a woman—without internalizing the constant onslaught of negative and unrealistic standards from the media and other places?

Key Term:

Body image: The *subjective* picture or mental image of one's body.

Too Much Outside Noise

In their book, *More Than a Body*, Lexie Kite and Lindsay Kite (2020) discuss self-objectification. They say we are not "inside" our bodies. Instead, we are "outside" our bodies, judging them, always looking from an "out of body" view. We think about what others see and constantly scrutinize our bodies through that lens rather than living within our body. Kite and Kite (2020) put it this way

The descriptors women give us of how they feel about their bodies. . .also reflect distance and detachment, as if the women are outside observers of their own bodies. It's that twin phenomenon,

*in which our critical, objectifying onlooker becomes the judge of
how we should feel about our bodies we live inside of. While your
body image is not something that can be viewed or perceived
from the outside, too many of us can't imagine our feelings about
our bodies from any other perspective.*

(p. 5)

We are conditioned by society and its messages to constantly criticize our body, always hyper-vigilant. Our body image becomes intertwined with how others perceive us. Body image is subjectively
built on layers of messaging, belief systems, memories and emotional needs.

Body image is subjectively built on layers of messaging, belief
systems, memories, and emotional needs.

I've heard over and over again from my clients that they worry constantly about what others think of their bodies. "Am I too big?" "Will
people think I gained weight?" "Will people think I look bad?" We
are conditioned to worry about others' opinions of our bodies as we
think about ourselves.

More than the Surface Level

Ultimately, body image, or our beliefs about our bodies, is constructed over time. We can have a strong and powerful self-con-
cept, or we can deteriorate into intense negativity. When working
on body image with clients, therapists see body image as a surface
level thought but built on something deeper. Body image is never
just about the size of your thighs or how your stomach looks. It's
about something deeper that you feel about yourself that is causing
stress in your life.

*Body image is a concrete concept to focus on when the feelings
we are having are more complex. When we project deep insecurity
onto our bodies, we miss the deeper meaning involved. Then we
have to work to establish security and confidence.* We are more
than a body. We *have* a body, and through its use, we accomplish

many beautiful things. Your experiences of your body and your belief about your body are a subjective experience constructed over time.

Your experiences of your body and your belief about your body is a subjective experience constructed over time.

The Three Contributors to Body Image

Our personal body image is impacted by three main things: (1) societal and cultural messaging, (2) our mental health and emotional needs and (3) family structures and genetics. Each of these interacts to reinforce a positive concept of ourselves or creates the building blocks of shame and negativity.

In her book, *You Are Not a Before Picture*, Alex Light (2022) describes her own recovery experience from an eating disorder and how she healed her body image. "There is nothing wrong with our bodies; we just think there is because we're trying to make them conform to a warped perception of perfection that is ever-changing" (p. 130).

All of us receive messages from society and from our families of origin. Those message impact our mental (and physical) health. We step outside our own bodies, judging, criticizing and creating layers

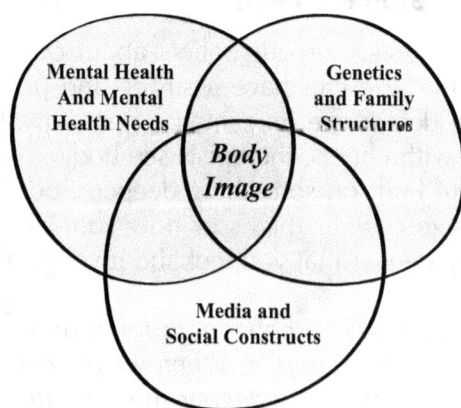

Figure 1.1 The Three Contributors to Body Image.

of self-loathing as we try to measure up to the "perfect image" we believe we should be.

It's a hamster wheel going nowhere and it's time to step off.

The Societal Origins of Our Own Body Image

Pause for a second and think about all the messages you have taken in from our culture about your own body. One research study conducted noted that 67.5% of the teenage girls sampled wished they were thinner (Robbins & Resnicow, 2017). That should shock us. That's two-thirds of the teenage girl population sampled! This is a systemic issue that needs to be addressed for everyone's well-being.

I have personal experience with feelings of inadequacy about my body, as do so many of us. If you've lived and breathed in this society, your story may be similar to mine. My first memory of self-hatred, shame and discomfort came at a young age. I was in the second grade, and I was at my friend's house. She and I were weighing ourselves for fun. I realized that I was trending higher than her, and she also made a comment about it, noting that I wouldn't be able to share pants with her anymore. It was such an innocuous comment, but it planted seeds of shame that would continue to grow in me throughout the next few years. As a child, she had no way of knowing that her comment would have a lasting impact on me. She had no ill intent. She was simply responding to the system that surrounded her as well. At some point, she received the messaging and internalized the idea that higher weights were "bad." (As a side note, the fact that there was even a scale available to use for "fun" also says a lot about the present narrative of bodies.) The culture around her dictated what she said to me, and I swallowed it down and it infiltrated my belief system about myself at a very young and impressionable age.

Fast forward to the following year. I firmly believed that I had developed "thunder thighs," a term that was swirling around my elementary school's social circles. A boy in my class called me fat. Those word and the self-consciousness they created planted deep seeds of shame—seeds that had already been sowed. It all had taken root. My beliefs were developing. In my subjective view, I believed that my body was bad and too large and took up too much space.

A mean comment from a boy in my class just reinforced what I had already begun to believe as truth: Large equals bad. For years to come, I would classify my body in this negative way.

But as I look back on these two experiences through the lenses of self-compassion and self-love, I see something else. I see that my body was not "bad," my thighs weren't "too big" and my stomach wasn't "too poochy." Instead, these beliefs came from our society—and they were just that: Beliefs, a story I told myself, but not a true fact. I was fed lies about what a woman's body "should be" and that the worst thing a woman could do was not to conform. We will come back to this narrative repeatedly in this book. As women, we are conditioned to shrink ourselves, believing we do not deserve to take up space both physically and metaphorically.

As women, we are conditioned to shrink ourselves, believing we do not deserve to take up space both physically and metaphorically.

Looking back, I wish I had been able in each of those situations to say that my body was doing exactly what it was supposed to—moving, giving me life and functioning for me. I wish I could have thought that I didn't need to fit into society's box in order to deem my body worthy. But I didn't understand yet that societal influences were dictating my beliefs about my body. At such a young age, I was not aware of the ways that the culture around me could tear down my beliefs about my body, especially as a woman.

Numerous societal factors influence body image and belief systems about the self. As seen in my personal story above, we are born with neutral beliefs about ourselves. However, our body image can become distorted as a result of negative memories or associations from past experiences. This could be as simple as my memory of a kid in my third-grade class calling me "fat," or it could be more complex, like living with a parent who constantly frets about their weight. Many clients tell me that the depiction of those with larger bodies in the media has had a specific and negative impact on their feelings about their bodies. Time and time again, clients tell me the shame it causes them to see larger-bodied characters playing roles that are caricatures. Throughout our work together, feelings related to shame and fear regarding body size come back to how they saw larger-bodied women portrayed as laughable or lazy. The culture dictated their beliefs about their body.

What occurs in our culture causes a dramatic shift in self-perception, often starting when we are quite young. We start with a neutral view, but once the messaging hits us, we use a lens of criticalness or judgment. Keep this in mind: *Body image is not stagnant; our belief about ourselves shifts and changes throughout time, and all the little or big messages that we're given create a portrait of how we should view ourselves.* After some time, our beliefs are not actually our own. We connect body image to the kid in our memories from fourth grade telling us we are too large or a fat-stereotyped character in the latest movie or a random picture of the latest actress who "got her body back" just three weeks after having her baby. We take in all these messages and weigh ourselves against them, most often believing that our bodies have fallen short of what they "should" be.

A significant contributor to these messages is the media. Later I will devote an entire chapter to media messaging. However, I want to discuss it here briefly because it has such a huge impact on how we see our bodies. Recently, I walked through a major chain store and counted no less than ten different negative messages about women's bodies in the store's marketing tools. Magazine covers displayed women celebrities' bodies, indicating who was "good" and who was "bad." Fad diet books touted the next starvation and deprivation tools we need to get our bodies up to par. Mannequins depicted body sizes that were not only unattainable but also unrealistic. How many times have you walked through an environment like this and been blasted with this subversive and unrealistic messaging? Think about everyone else taking this in as well!

Our society dictates how we feel about our bodies. The current culture informs what bodies are in, what bodies are out and how we measure up. Every day, we're flooded with pictures of what miracle diets and workouts have "accomplished." Scroll through your For You Page on TikTok or through any reels on Instagram and you'll be hit with message after message about reshaping, dieting or changing your body. We swim in a sea of these messages; we take them in and then create an unrealistic idea of what we believe we should be in order to be successful in our bodies. To put a level of pressure on ourselves and our bodies with this kind of unrealistic standard is incredibly unfair—and very damaging.

The Familial Origins of Body Image

Society isn't the only thing that dictates our body image. If you begin to peel beneath the layers of the belief systems about your body, chances are that you will also see a long-standing pattern of negative beliefs about your body in your family history. It isn't simply you who developed the distorted body images.

Think back to my first few stories about my own experiences with body image: Why was a scale readily accessible in my friend's house? Where did the boy in my class learn that "fat" was the worst thing he could call me? In each setting, young kids were handed a narrative from someone else that affected how they viewed their own bodies and others around them.

If you look at your family history, there is a high likelihood that you will see a generational component to negative body image. I can see the unfortunate lineage that was passed down through my family line, and it became particularly evident when I was recovering from my own eating disorder. It comes up even now as a therapist working with individuals with eating disorders. In my family, there was an emphasis on women's bodies and perfection around them, around shrinking and fitting into spaces rather than owning who we were. I have distinct memories of my sweet, beautiful grandmother telling stories. In every story the emphasis was not just on the facts or details of the who/what/where of the recounting. It instead involved discussion of how big her hips were at the time or how much post-baby weight she was carrying. It was the subtle, and not so subtle, messages that were consistently handed down to me. My belief about my body was impacted by the fact that I heard my grandmother discuss chocolate cake and how she loved it but couldn't have it "too much" or forcing herself to eat vegetables when she hated them.

My grandmother was a smart, strong and incredible woman. I look at her with so much pride for how much she accomplished and how fabulous she was. But I also see sadness because of how little she valued herself and how little self-confidence she had in herself and her own body. This wasn't her fault: This mentality was passed to her from her mother and others. Then they passed it on to my mom and then to me.

I hear so many stories like this from my clients. My clients tell me about their family members' own disordered experiences of their bodies—from mothers checking the mirrors daily to fathers mandating that the family will all diet in the new year to ensure that a child loses weight. In these and other ways, my clients recount how their parents' disordered eating habits created a disordered eating for them as well.

Research in recent years indicates that eating disorders are more hereditary through genetics than indicated previously. One study published in *The American Journal for Psychiatry* reported that those who have relatives with either anorexia or bulimia are 11 to 12 times more likely to develop an eating disorder (Thornton, 2011). As we have seen that anxiety, depression or substance abuse issues can change DNA and be passed down in the family line, we are also understanding eating disorder issues in the same way. As well, we are internalizing eating disorder messages we receive from family members during our formative ages. In her book *Mothers, Daughters, and Body Image: Learning to Love Ourselves as We Are*, Hillary McBride (2017) outlines her story of developing an eating disorder. She asks: What contributes to the development of poor body image and what helps our children not develop a negative experience with themselves? In her research, McBride posited that we inherit toxic messages about our bodies and may pass them on to our daughters, as they were passed on to us, without even knowing it.

When talking about body image and eating issues, to put it simply, genetics loads the gun, and our culture pulls the trigger.

When talking about body image and eating issues, to put it simply, genetics loads the gun, and our culture pulls the trigger. Particularly as women, cultural norms dictate our identity as being defined by appearance, by body image. We've been conditioned to allow others' ideals to dictate our value. Generationally, that was passed down from woman to woman in my family. The connection between my body and my self-worth was a constant. And instead of finding strong values of self-worth and security to find importance and self-esteem, I kept pressuring and pushing and worrying myself over calories and exercise. It seemed that those tangible numbers would provide me the value that I was *really* looking for. It's funny to say that now since as a psychotherapist working with body image issues, I know that it was never going to bring happiness. But that realization came with time and lots of hard work.

But these issues do not need to perpetuate in ourselves or in future generations. I read a quote that perfectly fits this concept of what we're talking about with generational body image issues: "If trauma can be passed down from generation to generation, then so can healing." That's the core of it. Families can have struggles; body image issues can plague generation from generation. But healing can also occur. One way to begin this process is by reading this book.

Shifting negative generational discourse about bodies starts with you. The work is to create the change of your own experience with your body—to create the future you. We can shift the system. We can say no to the messages we see that tell us what we have to be and instead learn to be OK with who and what we are. We can in turn pass this healing down to future generations. No longer do we need to shrink ourselves to fit into spaces that were designed to hurt us. We deserve to be seen and heard and to take up the space that is authentically ourselves.

We deserve to be seen, heard and to take up the space that is authentically ourselves.

The Connection between Mental Health and Body Image

Third, mental health needs and experiences are a key component in how we develop our body image. This is crucial to understanding how to heal from negative and dangerous thoughts about our bodies.

Understanding the criteria of what we are experiencing gives us the correct ammunition to fight back. Knowing the parts to the problem gives us the parts to the solution. Here's a useful analogy:

We need to understand the ingredients that make up the cake we're baking. If we don't have the ingredients and a recipe of how to use those ingredients, then we may end up with a cake that doesn't have baking soda and is flat. Or we may end up with a cake that doesn't have the correct portion of flour and is wet. Understanding the diagnostic connection to what we're experiencing gives us a name for the larger issues at hand. The diagnostics give us a basis for counteracting the corrosive nature of negative body images.

Poor experiences of one's body do not live in a vacuum; they are connected to and dynamically related to other co-occurring disorders. In the eating disorder recovery world, we often see poor body image as a precursor to the development of many eating disorders— poor experiences of one's body can initiate more compensatory behaviors which lead to eating issues. I am not indicating that poor body image always leads to a diagnosable eating disorder. It is important, however, that we understand the co-occurring roles so that we understand the best course of healing.

Poor experiences of one's body do not live in a vacuum; they are connected to and dynamically related to other co-occurring disorders.

Several specific mental health mood disturbances are more highly connected to body image disturbance. In the United Kingdom in 2019, researchers conducted a study to discuss the connection between mental health issues and body image. The study indicated that "just over one-third of adults said they had ever felt anxious (34%) or depressed (35%) because of their body image" (*Body Image Report*, n.d.). More than that "one in eight (13%) adults experienced suicidal thoughts or feelings because of concerns about their body image" (*Body Image Report*, n.d.). The link between poor body image and mental health issues is clear.

Furthermore, five out of the eight diagnosable eating disorders involve body image disturbance and/or poor experiences of one's own body as a criterion for the diagnosis. Specifically, these eating disorders are Anorexia Nervosa, Bulimia Nervosa, Binge-Eating Disorder, Other Specified Feeding or Eating Disorder and Unspecified

Feeding or Eating Disorder (Walsh, 2022). Not every person who experiences poor body image develops an eating disorder. But, there are numerous links between mental health needs and the varying issues that develop when we do not care for our body image and succumb to societal messaging.

A Word about Trauma

Trauma in its varying forms impacts our feelings and connection to our bodies. Correlating studies indicate that trauma can negatively impact our belief about our bodies.

Trauma experiences are widely present. Traumatic experiences interrupt feelings of safety both physically and emotionally. Research from the *National Library of Medicine* indicates "that a large proportion of people in developed countries have been exposed to at least one traumatic event in their lifetime, estimates range from 28 to 90%" (Benjet et al., 2015).

We understand from numerous different research studies that trauma is felt and experienced in the body. In his book *The Body Keeps the Score*, Bessel van der Kolk highlights the key components of how traumatic experiences impact our brain, which in turn impacts our mind/body connection. Van der Kolk (2015) denotes a dulling of physical awareness and symptoms related to traumatic experiences and an inability to connect with one's own body.

Part of the healing of trauma is learning to be back and present in one's body. Modern-day research regarding trauma reveals it is not only isolated to single, or even multiple, incidents but complex emotional trauma as a result from childhood attachment needs not being met. Our mental health, our body image, is inextricably connected to the trauma we experience in our formative years. Bruce Perry and Oprah Winfrey speak to this in their book *What Happened to You?* where they discuss emotional, behavioral and physical impacts of childhood trauma. In the book, Winfrey states, "The way you treat a child, from that time the child is born, is what sets them up to either succeed or struggle" (Perry & Winfrey, 2021). It's important to note that when discussing childhood trauma, we're naming not only physical abuse but also emotional neglect and dis-attunement in attachment needs. Dis-attunement in attachment needs occurs when a caregiver is unable to emotionally connect and care for their child. This may occur due to an emotional issue the caregiver is experiencing (depression, their own trauma, etc.). Dis-attunement in attachment needs can cause a rupture for a child to build a healthy, trusting relationship with their caregiver and in turn with themselves.

I will delve more into trauma's impact on our body image in Chapter 5. For now, it's important to understand that the healing of our body image is closely linked to also healing our personal mental health and trauma needs. The two are inextricably linked.

Conclusion

It's time to step off the hamster wheel. Together we will heal from memories, from messages and from the past hurts that have impacted your body image. We will rebuild a new way of relating and caring for your body. It takes time, but it is 100% possible. I've done it myself, and I've watched numerous clients do it as well. You can too.

Journal Topics

1 What would it LOOK like to feel free of your negative body image thoughts?
2 What would it FEEL like to be free from your negativity?
3 Do any fears hold you back from this?
4 What do you understand to be the connection between mental health and poor body image in your experiences?

Only Have a Few Minutes? A Few Key Points to Focus On

1 Body image is defined as our subjective experience of our bodies including how we experience them and our fixation on how others perceive them.
2 Data suggest that around 90–91% of women have reported experiencing poor body image at some point throughout their lives.
3 There are three areas of our lives which have informed how we experience our bodies and which create our body image: cultural & societal messaging, family messages and genetics, and mental health and mental health needs.

References

Benjet, C., Bromet, E. J., Karam, E. G., Kessler, R. C., McLaughlin, K. A., Ruscio, A. M., Shahly, V., Stein, D. J., Petukhova, M., Hill, E., Alonso, J., Atwoli, L., Bunting, B., Bruffærts, R., Caldas-De-Almeida, J. M., De Girolamo, G., Florescu, S., Gureje, O., Huang, Y., . . . Koenen, K. C. (2015). The epidemiology of traumatic event exposure worldwide: Results from the World Mental Health Survey Consortium. *Psychological Medicine*, *46*(2), 327–343. https://doi.org/10.1017/s0033291715001981

Body Image Report: Executive Summary. (n.d.). Mental Health Foundation. https://www.mentalhealth.org.uk/explore-mental-health/articles/body-image-report-executive-summary#:~:text=New%20body%20image%20statistics&text=Among%20teenagers%2C%2037%25%20felt%20upset,because%20of%20their%20body%20image

Kite, L., & Kite, L. (2020). *More than a body: Your body is an instrument, not an ornament.* Houghton Mifflin.

Light, A. (2022). *You are not a before picture: How to finally make peace with your body, for good.* HarperCollins UK.

McBride, H. (2017). *Mothers, daughters, and body image: Learning to love ourselves as we are.* Post Hill Press.

Perry, B. & Winfrey, O. (2021). *What happened to you? Conversations on trauma, resilience, and healing.* Flatiron Books.

Robbins L. B., Ling J., & Resnicow K. (2017). Demographic differences in and correlates of perceived body image discrepancy among urban adolescent girls: A cross-sectional study. *BMC Pediatrics*, *17,* 201. https://doi.org/10.1186/s12887-017-0952-3

Thornton, L. M., Mazzeo, S. E., & Bulik, C. M. (2011). The heritability of eating disorders: methods and current findings. *Current Topics in Behavioral Neurosciences*, 141–56

Van der Kolk, B. (2015). *The body keeps the score: Brain, mind, and body in the healing of trauma.* Penguin Books.

Walsh, T. (2022). Feeding and Eating Disorders. In *Diagnostic and statistical manual of mental disorders* (5th ed., pp. 371–379). American Psychiatric Association

Yes, It Is Possible to Change Your Relationship with Your Body . . . It Will Just Take Time

Myth Debunked

"The relationship I have with my body now is the relationship I will always have. Period."

I have worked with countless clients who walk into my office believing they will always hate their bodies. They've watched their parents, in most cases mothers, say negative and derogatory things about their own bodies time and time again. They expect that it's a hopeless cause, an effort in futility to try to shift the patterns that have existed in their own lives and lives of their families for so long.

But then I watch clients find peace. I watch them build a new relationship with their bodies. One study indicates that, among those with Anorexia Nervosa, 3 out of 4 individuals will make a partial recovery and 21% will make a full recovery (University of California San Francisco, 2019). No, you don't have to have an eating disorder to struggle with body image issues; however, body image issues are a component of most eating disorder issues. Understanding that there are individuals who recover is important so that we see that it CAN happen.

Just because you struggle with body image issues today does not mean that you will continue to struggle with body images for the future. I know the road is hard, the way is filled with two steps forward and one step back, but I've seen so many moves to a more caring place with their bodies. I know you can as well.

DOI: 10.4324/9781032654799-4

Let's lay out some realistic ideas about timing. You did not develop a poor relationship with your body overnight. It has been years of taking in negative messages as well as believing your own scripts of self-hatred. Family structures, cultural messages and our mental health needs have long affected our beliefs about our bodies.

Think about the first time you had a bad or unhealthy thought about your body. Can you even remember, or does it just feel like it's always been this way? Sometimes we can pinpoint a few specific precipitating events, even when we realize how present it has been. As you read a few of my stories in Chapter 1, you know I can remember myself beginning to believe my thighs were too big at the young age of 9, but I know the thoughts that I was too big were already there. I had an entire narrative of not being beautiful enough internalized long before I had a language for it.

I'm sure there are many parts to my story that are similar to yours. If that's true, locating the first memory of negativity with your body may be hard to do. It's like that ocean of "you should be better" that we've all swum in. Because these beliefs have been present for so long, it will take time to change them.

My point is not to discourage you about the time it has been that you've felt this way. It is to set realistic expectations for how long it can take to move away from negative messages you've internalized over a long period of time. This isn't an overnight fix, it is a process. But see the progress you're making and the movement that you're capable of making in the future. Just picking up this book is a step in the right direction.

Just picking up this book is a step in the right direction.

The power in this process is all about continuing to move yourself forward even in the face of feeling discouraged. That work requires a level of resilience and a level of determination. *Yes, it is possible to find peace with your body.* The time frame for that may not be as quick as you would like, but do not give up. It's like turning around a ship that's been running one course and headed in one direction for a very long time. It takes time to turn the ship and reset the course. That's what we're doing in this book: We are shifting the course. You are fully capable of this change.

Key Term:

Resilience: *the capacity to withstand or to recover quickly from difficulties; toughness*

Spotlight Story

Sherri is a 65-year-old woman. She had been battling with her body from the age of 11. She reported feeling extreme hatred for parts of her body, an inability to see herself as anything but reprehensible. She cycled through eating disorder symptoms for years running the gamut of binging, purging and restricting in an effort to get her body to be what she wanted it to be. It wasn't until mid-life, and releasing shame around her body as well as control over her body, that she was able to really make peace with herself. That came not because she found the perfect diet or exercise regimen; the peace came as she worked through the layers of self-hatred and rewired her belief system about her body in time. And it required continued resilience and continued fortitude to believe that she could actually make peace with her body and herself.

Body Image Develops Brick by Brick

Let's create another analogy around body image evolution. Go back to all those memories, words, pieces of feedback and internalized messages about your body from your past. Review them and think about them each as a small brick or block in a wall that has been built in front of you. As a woman in this culture, I know I could spend all day naming each of the blocks that have been laid, one after the other, in front of me.

There are so many triggers we can find ourselves surrounded with:

- Mean comments from others
- Having a parent who was obsessed with diet culture
- Fad diets
- Comparisons
- Shame
- Trauma
- The media's emphasis on looks

Any of you reading this book could probably add a whole list beyond what I wrote here. We each have taken in these overt as well as covert messages about what we "should" look like and what deems our body as valuable. Each of these messages has been laid before us brick by brick, like a wall stacked 20 feet high.

Oftentimes we don't even realize this wall has been created; each brick is laid without much emphasis on evaluating if we agree or truly believe what we're being told. Think back to the stories I told from my childhood in Chapter 1 such as when someone said my thighs were big and I took it, swallowed it down and believed it. Perhaps you can think of a story or stories you were given, subtly or not so subtly, where you took in all that was given to you without

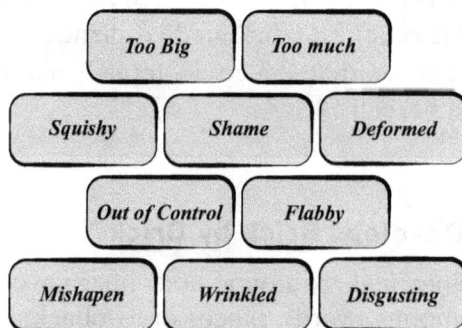

Figure 2.1 A Brick Wall of Negative Body Image Thoughts.

thinking through whether you really agreed. Think about if you really believe what you have internalized through your years. That insight and awareness is key.

When we realize that this wall has been built, it can feel that we are penned in by it, unable to climb it and unable to break through it. Take each brick down, sometimes one by one, and think about the history behind it, the idea if we really agree with what has been told to us. As you take each brick out, look at it and assess your beliefs around it (not society's beliefs or others' beliefs!). You will be able to discard what doesn't work. Perhaps you will rebuild something completely new and different, crushing the bricks that have been in front of you, the bricks that carry labels of "too much" or "too big" or "not toned enough." Replace them with gratitude or compassion for our bodies. Of course, it is no small task to tear down a wall. Give yourself time and compassion as you embark on it.

Give yourself time and compassion as you embark on it.

These bricks are made up of the elements discussed in Chapter 1 that construct body image—societal and cultural messaging and beliefs, mental health needs, and family structures and genetics. Think about the bricks I've described from my childhood—these are messages given by others in society, things that even young children take in from their surrounding culture.

Your Body Image Developed from a Young Age

Children are particularly susceptible to body-image-related messages that can either build strong or negative beliefs about their bodies. Hear a few times as an adult that your stomach is big: It stings! Hear multiple times that your stomach is big as a child, and it is a near impossibility not to believe and internalize this as something negative. Why? Research indicates that most of our core beliefs about ourselves are developed by the age of 7 (Fox, 2019). Who contributes to these beliefs at this point? Parental figures and other family members.

I really appreciate what Sumner Brooks and Amee Severson (2022) say in their book *How to Raise an Intuitive Eater*:

> In order for a person to develop their own inner trust, body appreciation, self-care, and self-compassion, they need to have received it from a reliable caregiver and had their needs met from an early age. Otherwise, in order to heal their relationship with food (and body) they will need to repair and revisit what was not established previously.
>
> (p. 153)

In this book, we're healing those memories, those core beliefs that were handed to us at young ages. We're changing dynamics so that we don't raise children with the same seeds of shame. *We're breaking all of those patterns*. We'll discuss more about breaking these generational patterns of dieting and self-hatred in Chapter 7. The main point for now—know that it is possible to deconstruct what messages you were given from your parents and to heal yourself and future generations.

Identifying Shame to Let It Go

It's important to pause and talk a bit about shame and its role in negative body image, particularly as we think about it as a brick that needs to be removed from the wall we've built around ourselves. I've used the word several times throughout the first part of this book. Brené Brown, a social worker, has talked extensively about shame reduction. In *Daring Greatly* (Brown, 2012), she defines shame as an:

> intensely painful feeling or experience of believing that we are flawed and therefore unworthy of love and belonging—something we've experienced, done, or failed to do makes us unworthy of connection.
>
> (p. 68)

I particularly love that definition of shame, especially in this construct of discussing body image and hurtful walls we surround ourselves in. When we experience something that leaves us with a feeling of severe negativity and unhelpful beliefs about ourselves, we can alienate ourselves from connection and from the voices and messages that would help us determine how loveable and desirable we really are.

Let's use an example here: perhaps your history involves bullying in your childhood. I have a number of clients who have experienced a history of classmates or others who said extremely hurtful things about their body sizes. These memories are seared into their brain and feelings. When we experience that kind of trauma, it can create a narrative that we deserve the disapproval of others. It becomes a stuck point in our psyche. Oftentimes, we become so stuck in this traumatic, shame-filled narrative of ourselves and our bodies that we no longer allow other more positive perspectives on ourselves. Our vantage point about ourselves is tainted through a lens of hurt and negativity.

Key Term:

Shame: *a self-conscious emotion arising from the sense that something is fundamentally wrong about oneself.*

Here's another example related to shame—you may be a survivor of sexual assault or physical abuse. Experiencing this is something that breaches the physical components of safety and can cause high levels of damage and disturbance in one's body. There are many harmful impacts that follow a traumatic incident, but this book is about the impact between our relationship with our bodies and our beliefs about our bodies.

Shame plays a very specific role in trauma. It reinforces a belief that we are somehow flawed or marred in a very tangible way. Healing can begin to occur when we first realize that we are, in fact, not unworthy or marred to an unrepairable place. Our bodies are beautiful beings that function in a high capacity to create safety in numerous ways for us. Because someone else has inflicted harm on us does not mean that our bodies are less worthy or less beautiful. This is the core belief system around shame that we want to release.

Shame does not get taken down very easily. Shame can block us in a myriad of ways. Shame is the small voice in the back of your head telling you that your truth is not valid. It's the voice disregarding your value in big and small ways and the voice telling you to be embarrassed of yourself and telling you to dismiss your worth.

In my history, shame meant holding on to words and language others had given me about my body. To use a personal example, I was told time and time again that my posture/shoulders were not good enough; "hunchback" is a word that comes to mind. Even as an adult, I had another woman, unsolicited, approach me to tell me that I "could be so beautiful" if I would just shift my shoulders back and stand more squarely. She added a suggestion for a waist trimmer that would help and an example of how I "should" stand.

Why do people think that comments or critiques like these are appropriate? It's because our culture is steeped in a sea of suggestions for what would make bodies, women's bodies, in particular, better. For me, the narrative about not being good enough was rooted in these comments about my posture that had started in childhood and continued into adulthood. Even in the face of experiencing that "feedback" as an adult, my first step was recognizing the voice of shame. If we don't call shame out, we can't do the work of refuting it and letting it go.

If we don't call shame out, we can't do the work of refuting it and letting it go.

We'll get more into dislodging these voices and challenging their words about our bodies in a later chapter, but for now, our important first step is acknowledging the role of shame in our lives. When we become better detectives, scouting out the shame-filled voice that exists in our memories around our body image, we are in a much better position to work at challenging that narrative. The work here is to focus on and recognize the negative voice first. The work is to recognize each of the bricks that we have built up around ourselves.

Calling Out Negative Messages and Thoughts to Rewire Your Brain

There are ingrained messages that take time to first see, distinguish and then change. I'm sure a part of you believes that it's possible to shift your view of your body; that's why you're picking up this book. Good for you for that initial step! Amid that, I encourage you to ride out the difficult times. Just because it takes time does not mean that it is going to be impossible for you. Brick by brick, memory by memory, narrative by narrative, you can shift your beliefs about your body and yourself.

Brick by brick, memory by memory, narrative by narrative, you can shift your beliefs about your body and yourself.

Body image is our beliefs about our body, not the reality of what our body is or looks like. If we change beliefs, we also change what we see and experience in the mirror. Here's a silly example: Let's say I believe that my skin is purple, and every time I describe myself or think about myself, I reaffirm to others and to myself that I have purple skin. The mind-body connection is so strong that I can even begin to think that I'm seeing tinges of purple in my skin! You are what you think you are. This does not mean that we lie to ourselves about what we see. But if we know that what we see has been skewed and distorted by negative messaging, we can work to shift our thoughts for recentering. There is value in neutrality. It has so much ability to change what we see and experience in our bodies.

Your brain has been shaped and wired by culture, family and mental health needs in such a way to view your body in a negative standing. We call this neural wiring, the pathways of networks of neurons in the brain that are responsible for visual representation. In everyday terms, we can talk about this neural wiring as being formed in a specific way repeatedly from all the memories we've been discussing. It is each of the bricks that has been laid in front of us. If your brain has been shaped by instances and memories that have given messages of negativity about your body, then your brain is "wired" to see self-loathing when you look in the mirror. But here's the really cool thing: it is possible to rewire your brain.

Here's the really cool thing: it is possible to rewire your brain.

It is possible to rebuild the wall built brick by brick in front of you.

Researchers have conducted fascinating studies of the parietal cortex and what occurs in the brain around body image, specifically when a body has been undernourished and overworked. Science shows that objects in the mirror (specifically our own objects) are not what they appear to be. Multiple neuroscientific research studies indicate the brain really can and does misinterpret what it sees related to the body and body image. Evidence indicates that the parietal cortex is the center for understanding, interpreting and processing visual objects. In those with disordered eating patterns, research showed there was abnormal activity in the individual's parietal cortex when shown images of themselves. More than that, lower serotonin levels in this area of the brain were also seen (Wagner et al., 2003; Mohr et al., 2009). Serotonin is a key neurotransmitter for a stable and happy mood, and it carries messages in the brain from nerve to nerve. Serotonin levels are lower in those with depression.

What does this mean? It's not the size of your thighs or your stomachs that are wrong. It's how you think about your body. Your brain is processing the distortions fed to you by a society, by a culture, by your family and by our diet industry that tells us we have bad bodies. If we sink into the next deprivation diet, we only make it harder and worse for us to see ourselves clearly. We now have actual evidence that our brains are literally impacted by this and unable to process our physical appearance correctly.

It is so important to note that neural rewiring is possible, especially in light of what I just shared related to the changes in our parietal cortex. You can nourish your body, rebuild your brain and rewire your neural pathways.

Key Term:

Neural Rewiring: *The process by which we create a structural change to the brain's wiring diagram*

It Will Take Time to Reframe Your Thoughts

These pathways that exist didn't happen overnight; it took years of memories, messages and internalized experiences about our bodies to develop the harmful beliefs we see when we look in the mirror.

Your brain can be rewired, but you have to give it time and tools to do so. On average, research indicates that it takes around seven to ten years for someone to fully recover from an eating disorder (Mallette, 2023). Longitudinal studies conducted on a select population of those with Anorexia Nervosa indicated that over a 22-year period, two-thirds of the subjects fully recovered (Given Time, Most Women with Anorexia or Bulimia Will Recover, 2016). While this may seem discouraging, you can find comfort in the evidence that you can eventually heal.

Creating a positive relationship with your body is possible—no matter how severely negative your relationship has been in the past or how severely involved with an eating issue you have been in the past. But it will take time, perhaps not as long as 7 or 22 years. The studies I include here are not to discourage but to encourage. No matter how severe your self-hatred has been, others have been there and, in time, found their way out. You can too with the tools we discuss and will continue to outline in Chapters 5, 6 and 7.

Learn to Observe and Not Judge

For right now in our journey, an exercise that can be useful, one that I've often done with my clients, is to practice becoming an observer of your body, rather than a judger. To look at your body and observe and describe without negativity is an incredibly hard task when you've become accustomed to those descriptors as being negative.

Chapter 6 will describe in more depth how we can first change our script to neutral. Our first step on this path for now will be to simply notice how often your language and your descriptors with your body involve self-hatred, judgment or negativity. The better we are able to tease out these negative voices, the better equipped we are to change the script in our brain.

This process of rebuilding a better body image takes time. I would pose that the process involves:

- Loving and honoring yourself
- Believing that you have the right to take up space
- Believing that your body can be valuable
- Believing your body is OK even if it's not perfect, or in fact, especially if it's not perfect!

To go back to my story above about messages I've received about my shoulders and posture, my work was to get to a point of acceptance about the way my spine is shaped and my natural posture. I'd spent the majority of my life believing that I had to change my structure, and in the face of someone telling me as a grown adult that I still wasn't OK, I had a choice to either allow the negative messages to be reinforced or choose to embrace my posture, to find acceptance in the imperfection. It was a process but I was able to reframe my thinking.

I am reminded of the client I discussed at the beginning of this chapter. At age 65 she found peace with her body and her food. Her eating issues began at age 11 and with a face of resilience, she didn't give up. Slowly and step by step together, we worked through key components and memories which contributed to her body hatred. It may sound daunting when you think through that span of time. But I encourage you to look at the freedom that came to her, that there is hope and possibility and that you can find that too.

So yes, it is possible to change your relationship with your body. It took you time to get to this point, and it will take you time to feel and think differently. But brick by brick, you can and will undo the negative messages you've been given and recreate a new script for yourself.

Journal Topics

1   Think through your history with your body image, the "bricks in your wall," and write down a timeline of messages you've received about your body. We call this the body image timeline.
2   Look back at the timeline and think about what parts of the messages you would like to let go of versus what parts are OK for you to keep.
3   Look at the timeline again. What role has shame played in your experience of your own body?

Only Have a Few Minutes? A Few Key Points to Focus On

1   It is possible to change and shift your body image beliefs. This shift requires time, resilience and continued focus.
2   The metaphor of bricks in a wall acts as a backdrop for understanding how the memories related to societal and cultural messages, genetics and family structures, and mental health needs create our beliefs about our bodies.
3   Our work is to deconstruct the messages we received and reconstruct a new relationship and beliefs with our bodies.

References

Brooks, S., & Severson, A. (2022). *How to raise an intuitive eater: Raising the next generation with food and body confidence*. St Martin's.

Brown, B. (2012). *Daring greatly: How the courage to be vulnerable transforms the way we live, love, parent, and lead*. Penguin Random House.

Fox, C. (2019, March 7). *By the age of 7 most of our beliefs and habits are formed*. https://www.linkedin.com/pulse/age-7-most-our-beliefs-habits-formed-carol-fox#:~:text=Psychologists%20believe%20that%20by%20the,especially%20our%20mother%20and%20father.

Given Time, Most Women with Anorexia or Bulimia Will Recover. (2016, December 16). ScienceDaily. https://www.sciencedaily.com/releases/2016/12/161220140917.htm

Mallette, M. (2023, July 3). *The hard truth of supporting a loved one in eating disorder recovery*. McCallum Place Eating Disorder Center. https://www.mccallumplace.com/about/blog/the-hard-truth-of-supporting-a-loved-one-in-eating-disorder-recovery/

Mohr, H. M., Zimmermann, J., Röder, C., Lenz, C., Overbeck, G., & Grab-
horn, R. (2009). Separating two components of body image in anorexia
nervosa using fMRI. *Psychological Medicine, 40*(9), 1519–1529. https://
doi.org/10.1017/s0033291709991826

University of California San Francisco. (2019, November 18). *Many patients with anorexia nervosa get better, but complete recovery elusive to
most.* UC San Francisco. https://www.ucsf.edu/news/2019/11/416006/
many-patients-anorexia-nervosa-get-better-complete-recovery-elusive-
most

Wagner, A., Ruf, M., Braus, D. F., & Schmidt, M. H. (2003). Neuronal activity changes and body image distortion in anorexia nervosa. *NeuroReport/
Neuroreport, 14*(17), 2193–2197. https://doi.org/10.1097/00001756-
200312020-00012

Chapter 3

The Media Lies to You

Myth Debunked

"If the celebrity/influencer can do it, then I should be able to as well."

Even the influencer in the post doesn't look like the influencer in the post. We need to continually remind ourselves of that fact. There are filters, Photoshop programs, AI images and more that impact what we see when looking in on a snapshot of someone's life. We can't compare our reality to someone's doctored up images and life presentations. Furthermore, we need to take into account access to resources and financial capital.

Celebrities have access to so much more in terms of products, interventions, the newest diet tools. Think about the Ozempic craze—it was the Hollywood elite that had the means and capital to purchase it in droves in the beginning. And this ended up setting the standard for the rest of the population. It's a mentality: if Oprah can do it then so should I. Not only is that unfair to us to hold ourselves to these unrealistic standards, a majority of the time it's impossible. And let's not forget that these influencers and celebrities are just people themselves, working out their own body image insecurities through products and extreme diet tactics. We don't have to buy into it (literally and figuratively).

There's a common phrase we often use in the eating disorder recovery world—"even the woman in the picture doesn't look like the

DOI: 10.4324/9781032654799-5

woman in the picture." We use this phrasing to remind people, and ourselves, that the images we are seeing on our Instagram feed or in magazines are incredibly different from the reality of that person's physical appearance. This is a concept we are starting to understand. Even a recent trend on TikTok has been showing faces with filters on and off, creating a greater degree of understanding about the different ways someone can present themselves just based on a simple click of a button.

In recent years we've seen movies made about the toxicity of social media and their impact, particularly on teenagers. *The Social Dilemma*, released in 2020, has a whole section devoted to the detrimental effects of filters and changes on social media platforms. Awareness is higher than it's ever been that the images we see are not accurate representations of what our bodies are. But even with this higher awareness, eating disorders and negative feelings about one's body image are more common. So what's the disconnect? Why, even when we know the image we are seeing is not true to life, do we still feel some level of pressure to live up to it?

We've all seen the Dove commercials. You know the ones: where women of all different sizes and shapes are hanging out in underwear and everyone is fully accepting and embracing of themselves. These commercials show an embracing of all different sizes and shapes, yet we are still struggling as a society to fully embrace our own selves. Ultimately, a few commercials and an exposé on the damages of filters in social media don't touch even the surface of what we've been experiencing as a culture for so incredibly long. Furthermore, we still see marginalization of ALL body types free of filters and Photoshops in these images. We have so much work to do.

Dissecting the Corrosive Messages in Media

Remember there are three areas of influence that make up body image: social and cultural messages, genetics and family messaging, and mental health and mental health needs. Our deconstruction work begins with social and cultural messages.

Let's take a cursory look at the history of expectations around bodies, women's in particular, in a Western cultural context. How women's bodies have been viewed in the past heavily weighs on what we think about ourselves now. We're zooming out, viewing women's bodies from a cultural lens to understand how these constructs impact our own beliefs in the present. This step is imperative before we jump into our specific tools for healing. We need to increase our own understanding for why we are so susceptible to poor body image beliefs about ourselves.

We need to increase our own understanding for why we are so susceptible to poor body image beliefs about ourselves.

Historical Standards for Women's Bodies

Victorian Era Women Embrace Conformity

Pressure to conform to body image ideals increased significantly in the Victorian Era. The Victorian Era began at the end of the 19th century and start of the 20th century. It was a time of immense conquest in the British empire, where it expanded its reign across the world. Aristocratic families amassed great wealth. With this wealth came power and with power came a further pursuit of who is "in and who is out" (a theme we will continue to see play out across time in body image issues).

Although body image ideals for women existed prior to this era, during this period of great wealth and opulence, the first body image trend took hold. We began to see a strong emphasis on women creating the "perfect" hourglass figure. The early 1900s were filled with women using corsets to completely shift and change shapes to conform to the ideal of what they should be. This type was labeled a "Gibson girl" after a male illustrator, Charles Dana Gibson, highlighted this body shape in his depictions of the ideal woman ("History of Body Image in America," 2016). Women were using corsets and crinoline to mold their bodies specifically into the ideal—a small 18-inch waist, large hips and broad shoulders (Tan Ngo, 2019).

While doing this, women were unconsciously stripping away their individuality, cloning themselves to look almost exactly the same in order to meet standards set by affluent, white males in order to be deemed appropriate and worthy of marriage. This even harmed their physical bodies, creating issues with breathing and decreased lung capacity and fainting.

Does any of this sound familiar? In today's society, we repeatedly see there is a new body image ideal, a new "trend" created and people, women in particular, shifting and changing their bodies to conform. The themes remain the same to this day but now the use of social media filters and new fad diets are the tools du jour.

We'll continue our journey through history to better understand social constructs of body image. But keep in mind this pattern we saw above—a dominant group in the culture creates an ideal of what the female body should be and in turn develops a hierarchy of worthiness surrounding this body type and women conform to the ideal body type. We've created a rubric whereby women are either "in" or "out"—desirable or unwanted.

We've created a rubric whereby women are either "in" or "out"—desirable or unwanted.

The cycle continues, rinse, wash, repeat to achieve a new ideal body.

White Standards Push a Racist Body Image

We can't have a conversation regarding the roots of body image issues in women without a particular discussion regarding the intersection of body image and racism. In her book *Fearing the Black Body: The Racial Origins of Fat Phobia*, Sabrina Strings discusses the inextricable link between the two. With the introduction and increase of slavery in Western culture, the white population found continued means to justify suppression. In an interview Strings conducted with Vox, she laid out the faulty line of logic and justification: "Europeans, primarily the French and English, began making the racist and pseudoscientific claim that 'Europeans have a great deal of self-control,' which gave them the right to manage not just themselves but others," Strings told Vox. By the same token, they claimed that Black people couldn't control their appetites, loved food and tended to be heavier. "This began the whole idea that Black people, as a race, were prone to what was considered a low form of corpulence that should be avoided," Strings said (North, 2021; Strings, 2019).

We cannot unlock our issues related to body image without also paying attention to the historical roots of racism and sexism that affect them. They have constructed how we think and how we relate to others' bodies.

In a study entitled "Beauty and Body Image Concerns Among African American College Women," researchers studied the direct impact of racism, both in historical and modern contexts, on body image in Black women. "According to Black feminist theory, the devaluation of US Black women is rooted in the institution of American slavery. Black women's bodies were routinely violated for others profit and pleasure without recourse or protection." The study continues: "Black women were viewed as hypersexual Jezebels (or Sapphires) deserving of sexual exploitation or as breeder women lawfully usable for populating owner's plantations with new slave stock or for the generation of revenues" (Awad et al., 2014, p. 541).

This takes us into a discussion of Sara "Saartjie" Baartman, also known as Hottentot Venus. Baartman lived in the late 1700s early 1800s and serves as both a symbol and fetishization of the Black body. In their book *Sara Baaartman and the Hottentot Venus*, Clifton Crais and Pamela Scully (2010) discuss the dichotomy that Baartman represented to the white elite in England and Europe. Known for her large buttocks and curved shape, she represented both the oversexualization and fetishizing of the Black female body and also the racist and dehumanizing of the Black body as well. Although Baartman's life began in South Africa, she lived her last years on display as a physical phenomenon in Europe, dehumanized and simultaneously sexualized.

I bring up Sara Baartman so that we can understand that body image, specifically body ideals, has racist undertones. It's impossible for us to create body freedom without also understanding how body image ideals have been formed and created throughout time.

In her documentary, *Killing Us Softly: Advertising's Images of Women*, Jean Kilbourne, activist and documentarian, depicts the history of the media, racism, sexism and capitalism. She reports and displays how women, specifically Black, Indigenous and other people of color (BIPOC) women, have been fetishized and marketed for big business's benefit. Sound familiar? We see the roots of it above with Baartman. (*Killing Us Softly 4*, n.d.). Kilbourne states in her most recent release of *Killing Us Softly*:

> Ads sell more than products. They sell values, they sell images. They sell concepts of love and sexuality, of success and perhaps most important, of normalcy. To a great extent, they tell us who we are and who we should be.
>
> (*Killing Us Softly 4*, n.d.)

I will restate this again: Body image ideals at their roots are a human-made construct. We see that on the micro level, in our own personal lives as we construct what we believe about ourselves. And as we rewind in history, these constructs occur at the macro level—in racism, in sexism and in power dynamics—which directly impacts our own beliefs to this day about a woman's body.

Sonya Renee Taylor (2021) in her book *The Body is Not an Apology* states it this way,

> Racism, sexism, ableism, homo- and transphobia, ageism, fatphobia are algorithms created by humans' struggle to make peace with the body. A radical self-love world is a world free from the systems of oppression that make it difficult and sometimes deadly to live in our bodies.
>
> (p. 5)

Key Terms:

Macro: *These are large-scale processes. Overall they are a conglomerate of societal norms.*
Micro: *This is an individual level of understanding and looks at personal interactions.*

Celebrities and Supermodels Present Conflicting Body Ideals

Let's get back to our timeline of body image ideals throughout time. Fast forward from the Victorian Era to more modern times, and we see the same cycle continue. The 1950s and 1960s ideals surrounding body image created two opposing ideals to follow—the Marilyn Monroe hourglass figure and slender, emaciated looks, as exemplified by 1960s model Twiggy. Both were very different in their idea of what represented the social standard of beauty, but both were harmful in the same way.

These ideals created a continued depiction of what would make a woman's body desirable. Those who didn't conform were deemed unworthy. What is most interesting during this time period is how two very different body types could both be deemed beautiful, but not variations in between the two.

Move forward from these time frames and we see a new "ideal" body type emerge—the supermodel era of the 1980s–1990s. Tall, perfectly toned, but still curvy. In this ideal, we see models like Cindy Crawford or Claudia Schiffer. At the same time, the rise of "heroin chic" emerged with models like Kate Moss with, again, an emaciated, stick-figure-like body. These are the same ideals as we saw in the 1950s and 1960s—two different extremes in body image types but nothing in between.

The most important thing that I see between these two oppositional ideals is that most bodies exist in the in between. The average body is neither perfectly small nor perfectly hourglass/toned. Most bodies exist in spaces that are incredibly different than the body image ideals we are fed from the media and advertising industry.

The average body is neither perfectly small nor perfectly hourglass/toned. Most bodies exist in spaces that are incredibly different than the body image ideals we are fed from the media and advertising industry.

Modern-Day Influencers Literally Modify Their Bodies Based on Trends

These prototypes continue to exist today. We can't have a discussion around the media's emphasis on ideal body types without discussing the Kardashian empire. There are links between all the varying ways we expect women to be able to shape and contort their bodies to be "worthy" enough.

The Kardashians are a multibillion-dollar family machine who built their wealth from the entertainment and reality TV industry. Their focus has always been creating perfectly crafted body image trends and styles. They dictate what is beautiful and what is sexy in body types. Are big butts in? Just look to a Kardashian to tell you. They have carefully constructed social media presences where they filter out any imperfections and set the trend for what is beautiful.

And yes, it does impact what we believe about our bodies. It is impossible to differentiate your own beliefs about your butt from what messages you absorb from social media platforms. Specifically, even in recent times there has been talk about how big butts are out and that the Kardashians have possibly removed their butt implants. The sheer fact that this is a talking point that many influencers have discussed shows how we have fixated on it as a society. As a culture we are focused on a body image ideal fed to us from a family with wealth and influence. This kind of influence is particularly harmful because they have also used their social media platforms to sell harmful diet paraphernalia—more on that in the next chapter though.

I was recently speaking at an all-girls high school on body image and the history of the ideal body types. I put up an image of the Gibson Girl from the Victorian Era and asked them to identify if it looked like any modern-day celebrity. Not to my surprise, many yelled "Kim Kardashian!" Of course these high school girls saw it right away—they've been taking in the messages being put out by the industry. We've been through so many different body image trends for women and they have cycled us right back to the sold waist-trimmer ideals. I call BS.

Cha-Ching: The Profits of Body Dissatisfaction

Why are we going back through history? Because we are conditioned to be dissatisfied with our bodies based on an industry that makes money from our unhappiness.

We are conditioned to be dissatisfied with our bodies based on an industry that makes money from our unhappiness.

It's the same with wrinkles and aging. If we were taught to be happy and feel secure in our aging process, a whole industry would collapse. The profit is from our discontentment. This has existed since the 1800s! When we know this, we are more empowered to shift our own beliefs. The more we realize that our beliefs about our bodies are controlled by an industry, the more empowered we can be to shake off these negative shackles and create healthier beliefs for ourselves.

I do still want to give credit where credit is due. In so many ways, we've come so far in body positive content, but the issue remains that even though body positive or pro-positivity images are on the rise, so are the opposing pictures. Social media has increased the number of images we take in on any given day. While we used to be subject just to the images on the fronts of magazines or commercials, now we can take in videos, reels and selfies nonstop. Even though positive body image pictures are presented, they are outnumbered by negative ones. And all are photoshopped and edited. On any given day, you are faced with a barrage of pictures, with filters and all of the cellulite removed, of bodies that dictate if you can feel OK about your arms. Though doctored, the images still have power and taking them in still distorts body concepts.

Think about the impact of this throughout your life:

- What messages have you taken in?
- Where have you been conditioned to believe that you are not OK?

Each of us learned these lessons somewhere. I remember seeing Suzanne Somers advertise her new ThighMaster machine. I was just a kid, but I was being told in those advertisements that my thighs needed to be shaped. A whole industry was telling me that I wasn't OK. If you look back, I guarantee that you will find similar experiences. There isn't a client I've met with who doesn't indicate the impact of filters and photoshopping on their body image.

It can be difficult to realize that our personal narratives have been shaped and rooted in someone else's—a whole other conglomerate's—opinion of what we should look like.

The *external* perspective, what we are talking about with diet culture and media, shapes overarching beliefs about oneself by dictating what governs bodies and sizes. It gives us a script to follow, a who's in and who's out, mentality. It can be hard to realize that this perspective, this idea of what we should look like, has been written for us. But once we pause and hear it for what it is, it's easier to do our own *internal* personal work. We have to identify macro messages we've received in order to do our own micro work to change them.

The cultural context gives us a perspective on why we believe what we do. It's not that your stomach isn't good enough—it's that the roots of what you believe run historically deep, even back to Victorian times. You are also told it is almost impossible to challenge them. If we're going to create change in our own personal beliefs, we must stop and realize how affected we have been by society's messages. You no longer have to conform to society's standards.

You no longer have to conform to society's standards.

Embracing Our Own Perspective

I have two memories during my own eating disorder recovery process when I became clear about the cultural messages I had received and the possibility of another script for me. The first came from India Arie's song "Video" in 2001. I still remember how the words ignited a belief in me that it was possible to break away from the focus on what my body was expected to be. She sang about bucking the system, learning to love herself whole-heartedly and doing so despite not being like a supermodel or having a perfect figure.

It was like a lightbulb went off in my head—it is possible to change the script. It is possible to stand up to the forces out there that dictate if you are or aren't good enough.

A second experience for me was reading Anne Lamott's *Traveling Mercies* and reading about her battle with her thighs and her own self-hatred about her body. I recall her learning to love her thighs, the aunties as she calls them, as she lotioned them up before heading to the beach. She was showing compassion, changing the whole way she talked to her body and herself. It was life-changing for me, a young adult who had only taken in cultural messages related to negativity and judgment with my body, to hear other people rebel against the system and express gratitude and love for their bodies.

What these two women weren't saying is that their bodies were perfect. The expression wasn't "I love my body because I shaped my thighs just right." It was an expression of "I can love my body even if society doesn't deem it good enough." I strongly suggest that you find a few of your own anthems (songs, scripts, meditations) to follow on this journey. It helps shake off the negative messages and lets you refocus on the power within you.

A bit of a rebellion is required. We need to rebel against the poor structures in our culture that tell us what makes our bodies good and what makes our bodies bad.

It is so important to pay attention to what voices around you are influencing you. Are you absorbing messages from Facebook, Instagram, TikTok or other social media platforms that tell you all about fad diets and focus on creating perfection in bodies? Unfollow, block and move on.

What we visually see matters to how we perceive ourselves. Think about where you can receive quality messages about bodies in your life. For me, in the age before a lot of emphasis on social media, it was in music and books. Perhaps there are people online who you can follow who can encourage you in the same way. Filter out the unhealthy; take in the positive.

Filter out the unhealthy; take in the positive.

I discuss this topic often in my client sessions. One client, a 19-year-old who had struggled with body image issues since she was young, had been strongly affected by the cultural body ideals. Throughout our work together, she would continually come back to ideas of what her body "should" look like based on the Instagram posts she saw from models and celebrities. She had printed out and covered her room in these "inspirational" pictures. Needless to say, these images did not provide the inspiration she was looking for but instead created more shame. Slowly, she began to see that using these images actively harmed her experience of her body.

We did a detox of her social media feed, removing accounts with triggering images. We added in body positive and fat positive accounts for her to follow. Just like my stories above with India Arie and Anne Lamott, we began allowing in those messages of rebellion that bodies in all shapes and forms were good. It began changing the way she viewed herself and the way she viewed her thighs, her stomach and the rest of her body. What we take in from influencer's accounts has a direct impact on how we feel about ourselves.

Here's the root of the problem: Whether it's body, lifestyle or personal changes, the pressures we face to continue to "keep up" with whoever and whatever cause much damage. So often we engage with ourselves from a cultural context of negativity without even realizing it. The work is to realize the negative messages that exist and begin peeling away those layers to leave space for the positive to grow.

Journal Topics

1   Look back at your history. What role have ideal body types played in your belief systems about yourself?
2   Cue to the present. What messages are you taking in from social media platforms, from advertisements and from surrounding influential people in your life? How do you see these messages impacting your beliefs about your body currently?
3   Where do you need to cut out or screen negative messaging? Where do you need to unfollow and delete the diet messaging that you're taking in? Part of your homework will be to do that now.
4   Keep a running list of all the negative things you've said about your body for one day. This includes off-hand comments made, thoughts you've had and more. I know this can be a daunting task to do, but it helps us create a baseline for what is happening in your mind. And we will use this for an exercise in Chapter 8.

Only Have a Few Minutes? A Few Key Points to Focus On

1   Media and cultural influences directly impact our beliefs about our bodies.
2   Body image ideals have changed throughout time. What is deemed an ideal body type is culturally dictated by major media

companies of the time and shifts dramatically based on fashion, diet and trends.

3   Part of healing from poor body image is being able to see, understand and call out the hypocrisy of the body ideal trends. We could go so far as to say that part of the healing with poor body image is to undo the brainwashing that the cultural messages of our time have dictated and created.

References

Awad, G. H., Norwood, C., Taylor, D., Martinez, M. S., McClain, S., Jones, B., Holman, A., & Chapman-Hilliard, C. (2014). Beauty and body image concerns among African American college women. *Journal of Black Psychology, 41*(6), 540–564. https://doi.org/10.1177/0095798414550864

Crais, C., & Scully, P. (2010). *Sara Baartman and the hottentot venus: A ghost story and a biography*. Princeton University Press.

History of body image in America: How the 'Ideal' female and male body has changed over time. (2016, December 14). *Medical Daily*. https://www.medicaldaily.com/history-body-image-america-how-ideal-female-and-male-body-has-changed-over-360492

Killing Us Softly 4: Advertising's image of women. (n.d.). https://www.killingussoftly4.org/streaming.html

North, A. (2021, October 18). The past, present, and future of body image in America. *Vox*. https://www.vox.com/22697168/body-positivity-image-millennials-gen-z-weight

Strings, S. (2019). *Fearing the black body: The racial origins of fat phobia*. New York Press.

Taylor, S. R. (2021). *The body is not an apology* (2nd ed.). Berrett-Koehler.

Tan Ngo, N. (2019). What historical ideals of women's shapes teach us about women's self-perception and body decisions today. *AMA Journal of Ethics, 21*(10), E879–901. https://doi.org/10.1001/amajethics.2019.879

Chapter 4

The History of Diets and How They Fail

Myth Debunked

"Being in a larger body size is bad for your health."

We are conditioned from our society, from our diet culture rhetoric, to believe that larger body sizes equal something unhealthy. But that doesn't take into account the genetically predisposed sizes that people are already set to be. The medical community has not taken into account that weight is not THE defining factor of health but is instead one of the many components that come together to look at health.

One of the main ways that we assess health related to body size is through the Body Mass Index (BMI), a truly archaic measurement system. In case you haven't already heard, the BMI was thought up more than 200 years ago by a Belgian mathematician named Lambert Adolphe Jacques Quetelet with no experience in the medical community (Devlin, 2009). The formulas are antiquated, the historical construct was never tested on any other races or genders apart from the cis-white male and it does not take into account the many factors that contribute to health. And this continues to be our medical community's "gold standard" for measuring health.

Weight, especially tied to the BMI, is not an accurate measure of health. Being in a larger body is not necessarily an indicator of being unhealthy. The two are not synonymous, just as losing weight is not synonymous with health necessarily either. Our society has created a fixation on numbers on a scale as the primary indicator of health, but our roots are rotten in this

DOI: 10.4324/9781032654799-6

concept. Two hundred years ago, a mathematician created a formula about how to determine BMI, and we've stuck with it to this day. No, being in a larger body size does not mean that you are unhealthy. We need a whole new determination of what actual health really is.

The history of body image ideals and the diet industry are inextricably linked and feed into each other. Why is this? People in power restrict women when it comes to body image in two ways:

1   Those in power fixate on women's bodies. If we spend time detoxing our bodies and measuring our thighs, we're not focusing on all the ways we can grow and evolve and create beauty and change in this world. Remember our terms macro and micro; the macro impacts the micro. The cultural rules for women impact our direct experience of ourselves individually.
2   Those in power focus on teaching women how to control their bodies versus how women can care for their bodies. Diets have been taught for years and years under the guise of help or clarity, but in reality they are simply a tool of subservience by the industry. We can't change our relationship with our bodies without taking a deeper look at our relationship with our food—the two go hand in hand.

We can't change our relationship with our bodies without taking a deeper look at our relationship with our food—the two go hand in hand.

Diet Culture Defined

What do I mean when I refer to diet culture? I'm referring to the norms and rhetoric around diets and dieting. This is what we're talking about when I explain the body image ideals from a historical construct—it's the ongoing narrative that has been used throughout the years to create a set of ideals that dictate what we believe is good or bad—who is in or out—in relation to our bodies. So a "good" body conforms according to diet culture standards upholding the cultural norms of the ideal body type of the time. And diet culture, the set of food rules that our current culture determines, tells us that we can achieve that ideal body type by adhering to the food rules we are told.

Another term I will use is diet industry. This is the myriad of corporations that exist as a behemoth of money-making entities that tell us what to do with our bodies. We'll explore this further, but I guarantee these companies do not have your body's best interest at heart—they don't even know the intricacies of your body's needs! What the diet industry has in mind is money and how to market the newest diet for profit.

What the diet industry has in mind is money and how to market the newest diet for profit.

Key Terms:

Diet culture: *A set of norms and language utilized to discuss the supposed right and wrong way to eat.*
Diet industry: *An industry established by companies who create and uphold new diets and diet rules.*

In order to heal our relationship with our body, we must also heal our relationship with food. A reminder about what we discussed about the parietal cortex—a malnourished brain cannot see its own image clearly. There is much research on the nourishment needed to be able to see your body image in a healthy way. Let's see how the diet industry and diet culture developed, where they're headed and how we can rebel against them.

Diet Origins and Evolution

The word "diet" has not always meant restricting food to change one's body. "It wasn't until the early 1900s that the term came to mean a restricted food intake to lose weight or change the physical physique" (Bberkley, 2022). Prior to then, diet simply meant the typical intake of food throughout a day. But around the 1890s saw the start of more measured approaches to changing the body's size and shape. A reminder, this was around the time of the "Gibson Girl." Advertisements began to emphasize body ideals more, the way for the concept of dieting to limit food intake for manipulating body size and shape.

Don't misunderstand me: Diet talk existed prior to this. Diet books date as far back as 1558, but these focused more on living longer lives, not on changing the body (Bberkley, 2022).

Diet Culture and the Diet Industry: Origins

One of the earliest diet books was published in 1825: *The Physiology of Taste or Meditations on Transcendental Gastronomy* by Billat-Savarin. It was a high-protein, low-carbohydrate-focused diet and laid the groundwork for what we now know as Atkins, South Beach and Ketogenic diets. Diets began to shift from being simply about what an individual ate in a day to how they could manipulate and shift their body and health based off food consumption.

One of the craziest diet concepts that we've seen historically was called Fletcherism. This was a fad diet that took over America and England during the early 1900s. In her latest book *You Are Not a Before Picture,* Alex Light discusses the insanity of this diet fad. People were encouraged to chew their food 32 times before spitting it out! Not even swallowing it but spitting it out! People had whole parties devoted to this. This gives us an incredible glimpse into the problematic behavior the diet industry promotes. Today, chewing and spitting food is linked to eating disorders. But in the 1900s, it was lauded as a pinnacle of health behaviors. Obviously, we can see here how our concepts of food intake can be extremely distorted.

The Diet Industry Takes Hold

To fast forward, in the 1960s, there emerged a strong emphasis on eating and how intake could change our bodies. It's not that this emphasis hadn't existed before, but there was a stronger emphasis on how we could control our bodies through food. The emergence of the diet industry, and how the media profited from it, became very apparent. So not only do we now have beliefs about what women should look like but we also have the roots of a whole diet industry, fueled by keeping women engaged with controlling what their bodies look like. Note that the diet industry profits from the failure of diets when people have to keep coming back for more.

A Different Decade, a Different Diet

The diet industry has pitched products and plans to convince us that we can control our bodies if we buy the latest and greatest product or sign up for the newest plan. The messaging can be dichotomous and oppositional: what's good/what's bad/what to do/what not to do? In the 1960s, diet drinks like Sego became some of the first diet products on the market. Diet pills such as Dexatrim were sold in droves. Time and again, various products promoted new results.

The 1960s even saw the invention of "tools" to burn or shake away fat, including "slenderizing salons" where women were hooked up to machines that would "shake" away their fat. (Petrzela, 2015). During the 1970s, the diet industry had frenetic growth. The media, specifically advertisement companies, used the concept of dieting to swindle people, specifically women, to "reach for a Lucky Strike [cigarette] instead of a sweet" campaign (Rotchford, 2013). The industry was always about making money from our discontent, not about actual health.

As eras shifted, the things diet culture deemed OK, or good, changed based on what new food, tool or even cigarette needed to be marketed. The diet industry's foundation has been to tell women what types of food or other products would make their bodies worthy.

The diet industry found its wings with the formation of Jenny Craig in the 1980s. This was the first multi-leveled system, a singularly marketed narrative that promised a way for women to format themselves into a specific look. Don't like your butt? This magical way of eating will fix that. Jenny Craig created a format of food that, if eaten in just the right way, would give the desired results.

Let's not forget how the diet rules have always shifted throughout time. Before Jenny Craig, flyers specifically targeted to women indicated that eating high-carb, low-fat diets would produce the results they always wanted. Fast forward from Jenny Craig and next we see Weight Watchers. Keep going and then we have the South Beach Diet, next Atkins and then intermittent fasting. Most recently, we are immersed in the clean-eating philosophies. None of these fad diets provided a way to care for, love and accept your body. All that they accomplish is a momentary feeling of success followed by the crash and burn later. Reminder 95% of diets fail, not because of user error but because they are unsustainable, limiting and unmaintainable.

The Latest Craze

As I write this book, Ozempic and other weight loss injection drugs have taken the industry by storm. These medicines, Glucagon-like Peptide-1 Receptor Agonists (GLP-1 RA), have historically been pre-scribed for type 2 diabetes; however, individuals are also using them for weight loss. Right now there are over 10 on the market with 4 being the preferred choice and highly marketed. GLP-1 RAs are medications that bind to and activate the GLP-1 receptors; these are incretin secretory molecules. This increases insulin secretion via a pancreatic beta cell, which slows gastric emptying and increases satiety. The reward responses to food cues in the brain are lessened, and insulin sensitivity is increased, which leads to weight loss (Jah-raus, 2024).

Sounds like a miracle weight loss cure, right? And yes, in some ways it is. People are losing weight; celebrities are touting its use. But like any diet culture pill, diet or miracle cure, we need to under-stand the greater implications. We must also understand that many of these diets and thin-focused interventions are reserved for the socio-economically privileged. These weight loss injections are in high demand with costs sky rocketing. Not only this, but also we do not know the long-term side effects to our bodies. These medi-cations create a dependency on them for a lifetime to achieve this weight loss.

Are the possible side effects worth it? Will weight loss fix our poor relationships with our bodies? Most certainly not. No injection or diet will fix the years of negativity that we've heaped onto our bod-ies. We cannot fix our body image by changing our body. In fact, we run the risk of creating another cycle of yo-yo dieting. Yo-yo dieting is the phrase used to refer the years long process of beginning a diet, losing weight on said diet and inevitably stopping the diet because it is unsustainable for long-term health. In yo-yo dieting, you gain back all of the weight lost. Lose the weight, gain the weight, this time with the risk of long-term negative impacts to our bodies. By the time this book is in publication, I can almost guarantee there will be yet another "miracle" weight loss intervention again. The cycle repeats.

We cannot fix our body image by changing our body.

The Harm of Diet Culture

The diet industry, the media and advertisers have never had your best interest at heart. They are capitalizing from body hatred, from the belief that your body is bad and must be changed. To be okay, you should be corseted. This is also where a strong overlap between cultural messages and family messages exists. Who among us didn't learn about diets from our parents? And, those parents learned about them from their parents. Everyone takes in messages from a culture that is fixated on thinness and focused on diets and the diet industry to "fix" us.

The rules about what to eat, how to exercise and how to present yourself continuously change. In the 1930s, it was all about grapefruits and shakers; in the 1960s and 1970s, it moved to diet shakes and diet pills; and the 1980s and 1990s saw the blossoming of the current diet industry's theme du jour—drawing in celebrities and supermodels as endorsements, the latest being Oprah and Ozempic.

But one thing remains consistent: if any of these things worked, produced the results of happiness and security with one's body being worthy, then the game would be over. The diet industry would have nothing else to offer. Done. Period. Take this diet pill and you're happy with your thighs. But that's not the point—the point is to keep making you come back time and time again to learn the new rules, to conform to a new ideal body type in order to feel secure.

But that's not the point—the point is to keep making you come back time and time again to learn the new rules, to conform to a new ideal body type in order to feel secure.

Try this new fad diet that promises inches off your waist. But it doesn't work. Never has and never will.

Here's the reminder for you: 95% of diet attempts fail at creating lasting weight loss. Oftentimes we think that this is the failure of us, the consumer, who doesn't have enough willpower or fortitude to stick with the diet at hand. Nope, not true. The failure comes into play on the diet industry end. The diet industry and diet culture set up unrealistic intake ideals for our bodies. Conversely, our bodies are set up in a way to operate at their optimal and healthiest place when they are fully nourished and at their natural body size.

Your Body Has a Natural Size

Set point theory comes into play here. What is set point theory? "The set point model relies on the concept of a genetic preset weight range that's controlled by biological signals. The body has a regulatory system that keeps you at a steady-state level, or set point" (Ghoshal, 2020). Each of our bodies has a weight that we achieve to be at our place of health. That set point has a range to it. This is a number that shifts over time. But I'll cue you into something very important with this number: It is not determined by a standard set by some major company in New York City. It's your body's own determination, set into motion by several factors including genetics and body type.

Key Term:

Set point theory: *The set point model relies on the concept of a genetic preset weight range that's controlled by biological signals. The body has a regulatory system that keeps you at a steady-state level, or set point.*

We need to be clear here though—the goal does not have to be finding and maintaining a set point in our weight for our lives. That's not freedom and acceptance for our bodies. If we're not careful, that's just another set of rules and guidelines that we can impose on ourselves, a tightrope that we end up having to walk to deem ourselves OK. I call BS and you should too. I approach the topic of set point to help us understand that we can begin to trust our body.

Trusting our body means:

- It knows what it needs.
- It knows how to care for itself.
- It knows the size and shape it wants to be.
- It stands in direct opposition to the diet industry telling us to control our bodies.

This might sound a bit radical, but I believe that our set points are much higher than we are led to believe. Fat phobia and the "wellness" industry have distorted this.

The Vilification of Fat Bodies

Fat bodies, those in larger bodies, are not necessarily any less healthy than another body. The fat-positive community has much to say about the concept of fat bodies being deserving of respect, honor and beauty. We have stigmatized and marginalized larger bodies. Remember our discussion of the roots of racism in body image? Fat phobia and judging of those in larger bodies is a power move. Who is better versus who is worse? Who is in versus who is out? It all feeds back to the diet industry and how money is made off of marginalizing certain body types.

Aubrey Gordon (2020), activist and author, has mic-drop moments in her book *What We Don't Talk About When We Talk About Fat*. One specific portion sticks out to me:

> We can build a world in which fat bodies are valued and supported just as much as thin ones. While body positivity seems to be everywhere, it doesn't appear to be changing our deeply held, deeply harmful beliefs about fatness and fat people.
>
> (p. 5)

She goes on:

> All of us deserve better than what thinness takes. We deserve a new paradigm of health: one that acknowledges its multifaceted nature and holds t-cell counts and blood pressure alongside mental health and chronic illness management. We deserve a paradigm of personhood that does not make size or health a prerequisite for dignity and respect. We deserve more places for thin people to heal from the endless social messages that tell them at once that their bodies will never be perfect enough to be beautiful and simultaneously that their bodies make them inherently superior to fatter people. . . . We deserve to see each other as we are so that we can hear each other. And the perfect, unreachable standard of thinness is taking that from us.
>
> (Gordon, 2020, p. 69)

Healthy Does Not Equal Thin

Oftentimes when I'm speaking on these issues, inevitably someone will say to me, "But Johanna, what about health? It's not healthy to be fat." To that I usually start by talking about the many, many, many unhealthy and extreme diet tactics that create severe imbalances in our bodies. The "Egg Diet" comes to mind, which made its rounds not too long ago. There are many different versions of this diet, but the main one being praised in the diet industry was the recommendation that individuals live off of multiple eggs during the day, with only lean meats and a low carbohydrate meal in the evening. It encourages individuals to follow it strictly, thus losing up to 24 pounds in two weeks. Are you going to tell me that that is healthy? Extreme yo-yo dieting with gaps in nutritional needs? Nope, no way. Our society is fixated on a thinness ideal to deem health and then engages in the most unhealthy behaviors to achieve it.

The Many Limitations of the Body Mass Index Scale

A word about the Body Mass Index (BMI). The BMI is an antiquated tool that the medical community continues to use as a primary measurement of health. It was created in the 1800s by a Belgian male, Adolphe Quetelet. The measurement was only conducted on other white males, and the standards which deemed health and size did not take into account various races or genders (Humphreys, 2010).

Only recently, in 2023, did the American Medical Association vocalize the concerns many activists have already been stating—the BMI is an unreliable measure of health and has limitations for many different races, ages and genders. However, instead of throwing out the measure, the association instead determined that it was still usable and could be considered in addition to other measures in order to create a "clear" picture of health—including but not limited to waist circumference (Berg, 2023). Instead of specifically recognizing and undoing the harm created by a racist and biased measurement scale, it was instead upheld with a "yes, and" clause.

Spotlight Story

I cannot even begin to tell you the number of clients I have seen who have been harmed by the measures of "health" such as BMI or the like from the medical community. One such client specifically comes to mind, Joan. Joan came to me seeking help for body acceptance and also let me know that she had been a chronic dieter since the age of 14. At the time of our first appointment, she was 58 years old. That's 44 years of extreme dieting. She kept her weights, calories and numbers all noted in a notebook at younger ages, a spreadsheet now in her later years. And where had all of this gotten her? In a body that the medical community deemed "obese" by BMI standards. She was tired of listening to the next diet guru who told her what to do. And she was sure as hell tired of being told by doctors to lose weight and that any other ailment she had would be "cured." The medical industry only saw her as a number on a scale and judged her as worthy or unworthy based solely on that number.

And then she experienced something I know many of my clients have also gone through, and maybe you can recognize yourself in this situation. She went to the doctor to ask about medicine for anxiety and came out with a script for weight loss. Make it make sense! It doesn't.

Through our work together, Joan began to understand the cycles of chronic dieting kept her in a box of self-hatred. She began to understand that the things the medical community told her to do to "fix" her BMI or her body were just another step in a long line of problematic messages she had been given about her body. We threw out the diet plans and worked on acceptance. We tossed the judgments and worked on allowing her body to take up space. And guess what? She feels the strongest and the healthiest she's ever felt. She still occupies the world in a larger body. And this larger body can feed and nourish itself with whatever it needs. This larger body can accomplish triathlons. This larger body exists and moves and functions for her. She stopped fighting against it and started taking care of and honoring it and that has been literally life-changing for her.

The Health At Every Size Movement

The Health At Every Size (HAES) movement as a concept has existed since the 1960s and 1970s. Several authors and activists have written articles about discrimination against fat people and backward ideas about health. One such article, written by Lew Louderback (1967) for the *Saturday Evening Post* was entitled "More People Should Be Fat." Louderback argued against diet culture, indicating that extreme diets cause emotional distress, severe and unhealthy weight fluctuations and negative impacts on individuals. Lindo Bacon published *Health at Every Size: The Surprising Truth About Your Weight* in 2010 as an answer to the constant onslaught of diets being lauded throughout the culture.

The movement has changed and shifted throughout time, but at its core, the principles have remained the same: Health should be accessible to ALL body types, not just those in smaller bodies. And, the number on the scale is not the only identifying indicator of health; in fact, it may be a pretty poor one at that. The focus of the HAES movement is on actual health, rather than weight and BMI.

Moving Past Never Enough

So why am I pausing to focus on the fat positivity movement and HAES? Because to heal from body image issues, we have to come to terms with the fact that we can no longer place society's standards of body image ideals onto it. We must come to terms with the fat phobic rhetoric we have learned and believed. And make space to change or view point on health. Furthermore, we cannot fall victim to the diet industry's allure of "fixing" our stomachs or our thighs.

To heal our poor body image, we must unravel ourselves from diets and diet culture rules. This may involve increasing your food intake—if you find yourself struggling to allow your body to have three meals (or more!) a day or limiting specific types of foods, I advise seeking the help of a dietitian who is educated in the underlying principles surrounding eating and recovery needs. Why do I say this? Healing a negative body image is not going to happen if you are under nourishing yourself, buying into the latest diet or dictating a number on a scale for your body. This is like trying to clean out your house while actively throwing ketchup and dust everywhere.

The two are in complete conflict. You cannot come to a strong and powerful position surrounding your body while holding on to rules and rhetoric that harm you. One side will win you over.

> To heal our poor body image, we must unravel ourselves from the diets and from the diet culture rules.

To recap, the diet industry does not have your best interest at heart. It exists as a means of creating money for those in power. It keeps us stuck in discontentment and fuels unrealistic body image ideals. To heal our poor body image, we need to come to terms with our unhealthy relationship to food and restore connection to our bodies' needs. You deserve to take up space—your body, your needs, your desires and your appetite.

Journal Topics

1   Write down your history with diets. Does it look like you've historically attempted to use diets to make you feel better about your body?
2   What would it look like to fully nourish your body? Do you have an understanding of what that might be? If you need extra help, you can look for a skilled dietitian in your area. One great resource to start with if you need guidance is Project Heal located in the Northeast United States (https://www.theprojectheal.org/outpatient-providers-by-region).
3   Are there any fears that hold you back from this? What might those be? Write them down and we will face them one by one in Chapter 6.

Only Have a Few Minutes? A Few Key Points to Focus On

1   Diet culture, a set of norms and language utilized to discuss what is the right and wrong way to eat, has created unrealistic ideals of food intake and body ideals.
2   Diet industry, a multibillion-dollar industry established by companies who create and uphold new diets and rules, capitalizes and makes money off of body hatred.

3   Diet culture rules have changed and have frenetically shifted throughout time.
4   The BMI scale is an outdated measurement tool for determining health created more than 200 years ago by a Belgian mathematician.
5   We need a deconstruction of what we deem healthy versus unhealthy and to move away from fat-phobic rhetoric when discussing health.

References

Bacon, L. (2010). *Health at every size: The surprising truth about your weight*. BenBella Books.

Bberkley. (2022, April 21). Diet culture: A brief history—The social and health research center. *The Social and Health Research Center*. https://sahrc.org/2022/04/diet-culture-a-brief-history

Berg, S. (2023, June 14). AMA: Use of BMI alone is an imperfect clinical measure. American Medical Association. https://www.ama-assn.org/delivering-care/public-health/ama-use-bmi-alone-imperfect-clinical-measure

Devlin, K. (2009, July 4). Top 10 reasons why the BMI is bogus. *NPR*. https://www.npr.org/templates/story/story.php?storyId=106268439

Ghoshal, M. G. R. (2020, March 19). What you need to know about set point theory. *Healthline*. https://www.healthline.com/health/set-point-theory#body-weight-set-point

Gordon, A. (2020). *What we don't talk about when we talk about fat*. Beacon Press.

Humphreys, S. (2010). The unethical use of BMI in contemporary general practice. *British Journal of General Practice, 60*(578), 696–697. https://www.ncbi.nlm.nih.gov/pmc/articles/PMC2930234/

Jahraus, J. (2024, March 21). *Semaglutide magic: Weight loss made easy perils for eating disorder patients*. International Association of Eating Disorder Annual Conference, Miami, FL.

Light, A. (2022). *You are not a before picture: How to finally make peace with your body, for good*. HarperCollins UK.

Louderback, L. (1967, November 4). More people should be fat. The Saturday Evening Post.

Petrzela, N.M. (2015, September 5). Slenderizing salons, reducing machines, and other hot fitness crazes of 75 years ago. Well and *Good*.

Rotchford, L. (2013, February 3). Diets through history: The good, the bad and the scary. *Health.com*. https://www.cnn.com/2013/02/08/health/diets-through-history/index.html

Chapter 5

Trauma and the Body Impact

As you've already read, our connection and our relationship with our bodies are made up of so many different things—experiences, memories and messages we've taken in from family and culture. Each of these things falls under one of the three umbrellas we've

DOI: 10.4324/9781032654799-7

discussed: societal and cultural messages, family and genetics, mental health and mental health needs. Amidst all these inputs, there are opportunities for our belief systems and connection with our body to be built up or to be torn down. To refer back to an earlier metaphor, there are opportunities for our body image to be built with bricks that strengthen our connection to our body and its needs or bricks that harm and interrupt our connection to it.

In this chapter and the next we talk about very specific interrupters, those occurrences in our mind, body and experiences that create disconnection with our body. Many of these interrupters are things that breach our safety. I classify these experiences under the umbrella of things that have been traumatic for us. This requires knowing more about trauma. Trauma causes an interruption in our connection with our bodies in various ways. I have touched on this topic in previous chapters, but now it's time to go deeper.

Even if you believe you have not experienced something traumatic in your life, I encourage you to read on. Chances are there may be parts of what we are discussing that will resonate with your experiences, whether that be from a single situation or ongoing experiences. In my work as an eating disorder therapist, many clients are startled to uncover traumatic experiences that have affected their beliefs about their bodies. They come into therapy thinking only about their body but realize that so many memories and experiences need to be healed to bring back connection and respect for their bodies. Read on and see what resonates for you.

Trauma and Body Image

In her book, *Unbroken: The Trauma Response Is Never Wrong: And Other Things You Need to Know to Take Back Your Life*, Mary Catherine McDonald (2023) says the following:

> Too often we think of trauma in terms of what happened—like an attack, a natural disaster, a serious accident or illness, a war, or a loss. What if, instead, we thought about trauma in terms of the reaction an experience causes?
>
> Something is potentially traumatic when it overwhelms the nervous system enough to cause our emergency coping mechanisms to kick into gear.

These mechanisms are designed to save our lives—and they do. But to do so, they pull energy and resources from some of our other systems, including those that help us orient ourselves in the world and organize our memories.

(p. 7)

I particularly love McDonald's (2023) descriptor because it highlights a major difference in how the world of psychology used to think about trauma versus the more recent view. Specifically, trauma responses are protective; trauma responses are about survival for the mind and body. A disconnection is created in our bodies when a trauma is felt and experienced, but that is not necessarily a negative thing. That is a protective mechanism meant to help our bodies stabilize and survive.

Key Term:

Trauma: *The emotional response to a jarring event or series of events that impact mental and physical health.*

Different Types of Trauma

A word about different types of trauma. Trauma is typically classified into three specific categories:

- Acute
- Chronic
- Complex

Acute trauma is classified as a single, distressing experience that breached the limits of safety for a person, such as a natural disaster, single episode assault or an accident (Allarakha, 2024). Chronic trauma experiences are "multiple, long-term, and/or prolonged distressing, traumatic events over an extended period" (Allarakha, 2024) such as bullying, domestic abuse or having served in an active war. Complex trauma is a reaction to undergoing varied and sustained experiences of trauma throughout one's life. It is typically associated with interpersonal relationships and has a severe impact on relationships others establish in the future. "It may be seen in individuals who have been victims of childhood abuse, neglect, domestic violence, family disputes, and other repetitive situations, such as civil unrest" (Allarakha, 2024).

I can't stress this enough: Each type of trauma is valid, and each type of trauma produces a breach in safety, both mentally and physically, for the individual who experienced it. Trauma does not only impact our mind but is also a state that impacts experiences somatically, i.e. how your body feels.

Reminder: We are traversing the difficult topics of trauma and mental health needs in an effort to understand specifically what impacts our connection and belief systems with our bodies. Healing our body image, healing our relationship with our body, does not come from changing our body—it comes from understanding and exploring these underlying experiences and healing our wounds, trauma included.

Healing our body image, healing our relationship with our body, does not come from changing our body—it comes from understanding and exploring these underlying experiences and healing our wounds, trauma included.

Trauma Stems from the Body's Defense Mechanisms

To return to what McDonald (2023) said, trauma responses are naturally occurring experiences in our body that are meant to protect us. The clinical diagnosis for these trauma responses in our bodies is known as Post-Traumatic Stress Disorder (PTSD). Specifically, if you've experienced trauma in your life, your mind and body bear the signs through

intrusive, unwanted images or thoughts of the event popping into your mind, such as when you are reminded of the event, tired or feeling vulnerable . . . the images can occur when you are awake as flashes of the event or when you are asleep as nightmares.

(Resick et al., 2023, p. 9)

These are referred to as flashbacks. This is also coupled with hypervigilance, a constant looking over your shoulder for the situation to happen. Both these responses are our body's way of attempting to create safety: Be alert, don't forget, it could happen again! It's not a maladaptive response but instead is one of safety and concerns from our minds.

Trauma Can Cause Dissociation

Another extremely important PTSD symptom that can impact our experience in our bodies is dissociation. Dissociation is defined as "a disruption, interruption, and/or discontinuity of the normal, subjective integration of behavior, memory, identity, consciousness, emotion, perception, body representation, and motor control" (Friedman, 2022). In other words, it is a depersonalization and derealization experience of oneself. To protect itself, the mind leaves the body and floats to alternate spaces and realities. This occurs when what we are experiencing is so traumatic that in order to protect us, we must find an alternate experience.

In all the symptoms of PTSD that we are discussing, there is a break in the experience of connection with the body. There is a leaving of the body as a means of protection. And this is important as it has acted as a way of keeping us safe. But if we have experienced any type of trauma response in our body, we must understand and have insights into how it impacts us in order to heal our body image. We must understand and have insights into the harm caused by our belief systems in our body in order to create compassion and care for our bodies in the future.

Spotlight Story

Jane is a 35-year-old female. She came to my clinical practice to work on binge eating issues. As we discussed her experience of herself related to her body, it became clear that her history with trauma was a key component in how she related to her body. Story after story that Jane recounted in our therapy sessions related to being bullied throughout her childhood—elementary school, middle school and high school were filled with memories of being picked on for her size and shape. Jane discussed feeling low self-worth and extreme self-hatred related to these experiences. She also noted having parents who reinforced weight loss as a means of protection around the bullying. Jane would be put on diet and, after diet, even sent to "fat camp" in the hopes that weight loss would be the magic cure for stopping the bullying. The diet would start, Jane would lose weight, but then inevitably, the diet would fail, and Jane would gain back the weight lost plus more. It was a shame cycle that Jane felt unable to break.

At the start of our sessions, Jane recounted the trauma history around the bullying, as well as the messages she was given about her body at the time. In her relationships to this day, Jane was hypervigilant for others to reject her; she felt that she had to control and calculate in her relationships to avoid being vulnerable and hurt, to avoid being bullied. And the same cycles played out with her body, one diet after another to attempt to lose the weight, and lose the memories, related to hatred with her body.

The diet plans didn't work when she was little, and they continued to not work as an adult. Real healing came when Jane, through therapy, explored the trauma related to the bullying and processed the healing her mind and body needed. Real healing came when Jane forgave herself for the years of diets she had sought and realized that it wasn't she who was failing but the diets themselves. Jane realized that the binge eating was in direct relation to a mechanism of hiding herself and numbing herself from the pain caused by others. And she worked to reconnect and honor her body, eating in a way that felt safe and good for her body and her mind. She rebuilt a narrative of her body that undid the messages the past bullies had given, and through this process she realized the ways she had internalized and lived out the messages from the bullies in her body.

How Trauma Affects the Body

Bessel Van Der Kolk, in his book *The Body Keeps the Score,* discusses the human nervous system and what is triggered during traumatic experiences. The two central nervous systems are the sympathetic nervous system (SNS) and the parasympathetic nervous system (PNS). The SNS manages the fight, flight, freeze and fawn responses that can be experienced in our body. The PNS is focused on slowing down our heart rates, relaxing our bodies and bringing us back into homeostasis (Van der Kolk, 2015). These are the components of our body that are triggered during traumatic experiences. And to bring this back to our body image discussion, the SNS is where the disruption and the disconnect first begin in our body during a traumatic situation.

I have my own story of trauma, specifically in childhood, which caused these responses. I had a parent who was like a ticking time bomb with their anger, and as a child the *tick tick tick* toward anger was palpable. My central nervous system could feel it, and when the agitation from that parent began to turn to anger, I could feel my heart rate rising and myself panicking. My SNS was in full swing, without me realizing what it was. There were racing thoughts of how to get out of the situation. And in those moments, as I look back, the disconnection from my body was clear. I would do anything to leave those situations, to leave my body. Maybe this resonates with you as well. Maybe you've developed your own form of escapism. And if this is the case, the experiences that we have in body image NOW are centrally connected to that past disconnect that was created during these young ages. These are our roots of leaving our body as a protective mechanism.

Embodiment, Trauma and Body Image

Our belief systems about our body end up being the embodiment of the trauma. Body image, aka our subjective experience of our body, is at the surface to something deeper. I couldn't control the anger I experienced from my parent; I couldn't stop it from happening or escape it. But what I could do was numb out from it by focusing on the size of my stomach or the number on the scale. It was a way of controlling a very out-of-control situation I found myself in as a young child. Go back to the story above about my client Jane

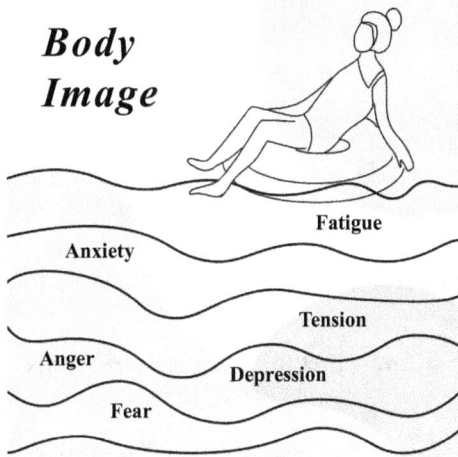

Figure 5.1 What's Underneath Our Body Image.

and her experiences with bullying. She couldn't stop the bullies, but she could attempt to shrink her body to make it unseen. She couldn't stop the comments from her parents, but she could work to make her body something more pleasing to them to decrease their chastisements.

We need to honor those parts of ourselves that worked to protect our minds and our bodies. Dieting and attempting to change your body may have provided a level of safety at some time in your life. To diminish the need and importance of that is to diminish our experiences.

Trauma Relates to Safety and Connection

Jasmin Lee Cori (2017) writes extensively about the topic of attachment trauma and the places in our childhood and upbringing where we experienced a breach in safety and connection with our primary caregivers. In her book *The Emotionally Absent Mother: How to Recognize and Heal the Invisible Effects of Childhood Emotional Neglect,* she explores all the various ways that having a caregiver who is unstable emotionally and inconsistent can impact your belief systems about yourself. She specifically outlines how the disconnect we discussed above causes a rupture in our ability to be in tune with our body and its needs. "Not occupying the body fully makes it harder for the body to thrive. The body is separated from the energetic matrix it takes instruction from" (Cori, 2017, p. 118).

If you grew up in a family where your emotional needs were constantly dismissed or discredited, there is a high likelihood that attunement and connection to your body were interrupted. And there is an equally high possibility that your experience of your body, your body image, has been interrupted related to this trauma.

Creating Physical and Emotional Safety to Heal Body Image

In the second part of this book, we embark on healing and connecting again to our bodies. When we do this, it is of utmost importance that both physical and emotional safety are established for yourself. What that looks like depends on what traumatic experiences existed in your past. However, no matter what, physical safety must be created and maintained. If you are still connected to someone who physically or emotionally harmed you, your body will bear the impact. Reestablishing connection to your body and realigning yourself in attunement to what it needs will prove to be much more difficult.

Trauma and Shame

We can develop shame about our bodies and ourselves when we experience a traumatic event. We touched on this in Chapter 2 when discussing the bricks in our wall. Experiencing trauma impacts our belief systems about ourselves and leaves us feeling disconnected and shameful in our own minds and bodies. We come to believe we are to blame for what happened and that we are not good enough or did not protect ourselves well enough, ultimately thinking our bodies are bad because of the trauma.

This is one significant way that our body image belief systems are interrupted when trauma has occurred. We carry the negative belief systems with us, we carry the shame. We disconnect and numb our bodies, believing that they need to be quieted or controlled rather than felt and believed. We bear the effects of shame rather than releasing it. Please understand that healing your relationship with your body, if you've experienced trauma of any kind throughout your life, begins with healing the traumatic memories and establishing trust with your mind/body connection again.

Our bodies are not bad; our bodies do not deserve the shame and negativity that have been brought upon them through these experiences. Understanding this is the first step in healing our body image. However, this healing for our body image cannot only occur in our thoughts. The thoughts are less than half the story of what we believe about our body. Healing our body image also begins with healing the trauma that is trapped in our bodies.

Releasing Trauma

In his book, *My Grandmother's Hands: Racialized Trauma and the Pathway to Mending Our Hearts and* Bodies, Resmaa Menakem (2017) discusses the importance of releasing trauma from not only our minds but our bodies. He discusses the impact of trauma, specifically intergenerational racial trauma and healing. His book is pivotal in the world of racial justice. One tool that he discusses for healing is specifically important for the work we are embarking on in our journey to heal body image, which is completing the action that was thwarted. Menakem refers to this as an "action completion." "This releases the trauma energy stuck in your body. You can then use this energy to metabolize the trauma" (Menakem, 2017, p. 178). Our bodies must be stabilized and protected during these action completions; we must be very in tune with what we need.

Let's return to the vignette about Jane and the bullies in her life. Completing an action to provide healing in this situation may be for her to stand up for herself verbally when her mother comments on her weight. It may also be for her to fully nourish her body as an act of rebellion to what the bullies told her about her weight and size. I like the word rebellion here when we are talking about completing the action. With so many people I talk to, it is an act of rebellion to complete an action where trauma has impacted their body and body image. When we feel negative about our bodies, it is an act of rebellion to complete an action of self-care. Your body is good, and your body deserves this.

When we feel negative about our bodies, it is an act of rebellion to complete an action of self-care. Your body is good, and your body deserves this.

Showing Compassion Toward Yourself

Keep in mind this healing perspective as we embark on Part 2 of our journey later in this book. When we begin with the tasks and tools of healing your body image, you may encounter some of your own resistance to this. That's OK and understandable; your body has been internalizing these difficult messages for quite some time. This is a reminder to approach yourself and your healing journey with a level of compassion. The disconnect that has occurred in the past is directly related to establishing safety for yourself and your body. Reestablishing connection can occur and must be done with compassion at the core, as well as with a level of repair work.

One noteworthy item: I encourage you to do this with the help of a trusted therapist who can guide you through the healing journey. It is no small task to face trauma from the past. Establishing safety is key and finding a therapist you trust to work on these issues can be life changing.

Spotlight Story

My client Darla refused to wear shorts. She hated everything about her legs; she refused to even look at them in the mirror. She came into therapy wanting to wear shorts and change her thoughts about what her legs looked like. But what we first had to uncover is where she learned to think negatively about her legs. As we explored this, she recounted story after story of a mother who berated her constantly. "You're doing this wrong." "Why are you so stupid?!" "Didn't you realize that doing your homework that way would be the most idiotic thing to do?!" And finally, her mother said many negative comments that put down her body. "Your stomach looks so big, make sure you suck it in." "You're gaining weight, no one likes a chunky girl."

As we recounted these memories, it became crystal clear that Darla's experience of her thighs, her worries around her thighs, were in direct response to her mother's criticism of her. "Fixing" or changing her thighs was not going to change her belief systems around herself or her trauma. What was needed was a healing of the abuse she had suffered with her mother. As we worked through this narrative that Darla had internalized and as we healed the childhood parts of herself, the connection and response in her body slowly followed suit.

Anxiety, Depression and Body Image

As we've already discussed, our mental health and our mental health needs have a direct impact on our body image. There is a symbiotic relationship between the two. We see it listed in the *DSM-V:* A major facet of depression is weight loss or weight gain; severe depression can involve a complete disconnect or dissociation from one's body. Anxiety wreaks havoc on our bodies as we can feel the tension and worry in the PNS that is activated when we are struggling with increased worries. There is no doubt that the relationship between our mind and our bodies can be interrupted when we are experiencing more of a mental health crisis.

Remember That Our Bodies Cannot Fix Our Mind

We cannot look to our bodies to fix our minds. What do I mean by this? I certainly don't mean that we disconnect our bodies and solely work on fixing our mind—that is a huge disservice to the mind-body connection that we have linked earlier in discussions of trauma. But I have tried in early stages of eating issues to numb myself from the anxiety or fix myself by losing weight to fix my depression. It has not worked, nor will it ever work. The end goal cannot be fixing our

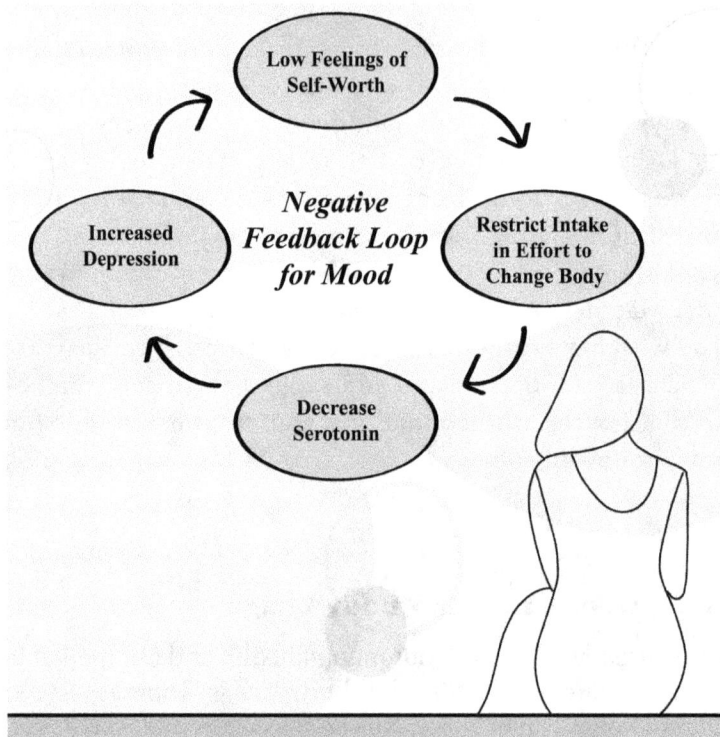

Figure 5.2 The Negative Feedback Loop.

mental health needs by changing our bodies. The only reason we believe this to be the "solution" is because we have been fed lies from media and diet culture.

The second part of this book discusses in-depth methods for how we create changes in our mind-body connection in order to produce long-lasting healing. For now, one of the most important things we can do is understand that changing our body won't change our anxiety, depression or mental health needs. It won't heal our memories of trauma. Yes, it does numb us; yes, it does shut down parts of our feelings and quiets certain components of this. But this does not bring about actual long-lasting healing.

In fact, we have a lot of data on how undernourishing our bodies can actually produce MORE anxiety and depression. A study conducted in 2018 noted that a decrease in serotonin was observed in patients who were experiencing restrictive patterns (Bailer & Kaye, 2010).

Healing our mind-body connection, getting our body and our mind readjusted and in communication with each other, is a key component of caring for depression, anxiety and trauma. This stands in direct opposition to jumping on the new diet plan or using weights and numbers to build ourselves up.

When we move into Part 2, "Healing Our Parts," keep in mind that reconnecting to your body may produce an increase in anxiety, depression or trauma memories. If this happens, it does not mean that you need to return to body-controlled or body-focused behaviors to cope or numb, although I do understand the urge to do this. Remember our self-feeding cycle—another diet won't fix your feelings about your body, and it certainly won't fix your anxiety or depression. If you find this to be the case for you, the help of a psychotherapist may be a key component of your healing. It is important to explore and care for the anxiety, depression, trauma or any other mental health needs that may increase related to working through body image needs. We cannot simply sweep the feelings back under the rug.

This process is an uncovering of many things. Take it at your own pace, but please vow not to return to the old ways of being. Instead, embark on a new path of facing and working through both your body and your mind's needs.

It is possible to heal your relationship with your body, and it's possible to care for and heal your relationship with your mind.

Journal Topics

1 While reading about trauma, did you identify any traumatic experiences you had throughout your life?
2 If the answer to the above is yes, what are specific "completing the action" steps you can take to begin to pave the way for healing?
3 Are there any resistant feelings toward completing the action? Take time to journal about that resistance to understand if it is protective or avoidant.

Only Have a Few Minutes? A Few Key Points to Focus On

1 Trauma can be classified into three specific types—acute (single incident), chronic (multiple, long-term and/or prolonged

distressing, traumatic events) and complex (sustained experiences of trauma throughout one's life, typically associated with interpersonal relationships and attachment needs).

2 It can be helpful to think about trauma not as an event that happened to us but instead as our reaction to events, relationships and things that have overloaded our systems. In this definition, we see our bodies as attempting to find equilibrium.

3 Our body bears the impact of trauma with hypervigilance, disconnection and numbing feelings as a safety technique for managing difficult memories and feelings.

4 Healing work involves stabilizing, grounding and reconnecting our bodies to our minds.

References

Allarakha, S. (2024, February 13). *What are the 3 types of trauma?* MedicineNet. https://www.medicinenet.com/what_are_the_3_types_of_trauma/article.htm

Bailer, U. F., & Kaye, W. H. (2010). Serotonin: Imaging findings in eating disorders. In R. A. H. Adan & W. H. Kaye (Eds.), *Current topics in behavioral neurosciences* (pp. 59–79). Springer. https://doi.org/10.1007/7854_2010_78

Cori, J. E. (2017). *The emotionally absent mother: How to recognize and heal the invisible effects of childhood emotional neglect.* The Experiment.

Friedman, M. et al. (2022). Trauma and stressor related disorders. In *Diagnostic and statistical manual of mental disorders* (5th ed., pp. 295–348) American Psychiatric Association.

McDonald, M. (2023). *Unbroken: The trauma response is never wrong: And other things you need to know to take back your life.* SoundsTrue.

Menakem, R. (2017). *My grandmother's hands: Racialized trauma and the pathway to mending our hearts and bodies.* Central Recovery Press.

Resick, P. A., et al. (2023). *Getting unstuck from PTSD: Using cognitive processing therapy to guide your recovery.* Guilford Press.

Van der Kolk, B. (2015). *The body keeps the score: Brain, mind, and body in the healing of trauma.* Penguin Books.

Chapter 6

Interrupters to Body Connection

Body image is anything but stagnant. Our experience with our body changes throughout time. What you felt about your body at age 7 has changed. Throughout our lives, specific events have very specific impacts. As we've already talked about, these can be specific bricks in our wall that shift how we think about ourselves and our bodies. Some of them even become like cornerstones, where we

DOI: 10.4324/9781032654799-8

hold up a whole new identity about ourselves and our bodies with them as our lynch pin.

Resulting from specific events, we may have a break in our experience of ourselves. I'm calling these "interrupters" in our relationship with our body. When these events occur, a shift happens related to how we see and experience our bodies. To note specifically, these circumstances do not have to be interrupters. They could potentially create a deeper connection and understanding of our body's needs. However, so often this is not the case. We are conditioned to interact and understand our bodies in one way—"this is how it operates," "this is what makes it valuable," "if your body functions this way, it's better." We are trained by a society to believe that our body's value comes from what it produces. Because of this, when our body changes or has an interrupter, it impacts how we connect with and perceive our body throughout these experiences.

Key Term:

Body Image Interrupters: *A physical experience in our life and bodies that negatively impacts our mind/ body connection.*

In this chapter, we will discuss more in depth those specific things that change our experience of our bodies. These life events can include:

- Illnesses
- Chronic conditions
- Pregnancy and postpartum needs
- Aging

Whether these events are things we're aware are coming (one example would be menopause for those in cis-gender female bodies) or we're surprised about (such as a life-altering diagnosis of cancer), these events change how we experience our bodies and ourselves. These events occur and create a marked shift in our own experiences.

Changes Take Validation and Understanding

A close friend underwent a double mastectomy at the age of 38 years old. This changed how she viewed her body, how she experienced herself. Another close friend had major reconstructive surgery on her back at age 44. This created a specific shift in how she interacted with her body. I've watched countless clients struggle with fertility issues, finally become pregnant and then struggle (and feel guilt for struggling) with the experience of their body due to how it changes during pregnancy. There is loss, there is grieving and there is a shift in our bodies when these major changes occur within it. It's important for us to validate these changes as well as understand why these shifts happen.

You may not relate to all components of this chapter. Perhaps the life events and physical changes we're discussing have not happened to you. But chances are you will find yourself in one of these situations someday. These resources could be helpful to have in your toolbox.

Specific Types of Interrupters and How They Affect Body Image

Chronic Conditions

The Agency for Healthcare Research and Quality (n.d.) defines a chronic condition as

> a condition that lasts 12 months or longer and meets one or both of the following tests: (a) it places limitations on self-care, independent living, and social interactions; (b) it results in the need for ongoing intervention with medical products, services, and special equipment.

In other words, the physical condition a person is facing is long term and places strain on their physical health. It is an interrupter in someone's connection with their own body. This interruption deserves space to process. Unfortunately, in our society and in our world, we end up judging our bodies and feeling more and more disconnected with our bodies during these difficult health changes.

Let's go back to the story I told about my back and posture issues and the feedback I received about my body then. I was told I "could be so beautiful" if I had a straighter back. I have scoliosis, a chronic condition that involves my spine and creates a curvature in my back. Therefore, I can choose to judge my back or to think about how to nurture my back. My life has been a process in letting go of standards of beauty to rebuild care and compassion for my body.

In 2024, I attended a powerful training by Tamie Gangloff, a therapist and on author on chronic conditions and body image needs. Gangloff discussed how chronic conditions can impact our body image experience. I left feeling so very aware of how we have not properly addressed the impact of chronic conditions on our body image. So many times, a solution to negative experiences of one's body is to begin trusting your body more. *But what does that look like if you've lost trust with your body because of health conditions? How do we build a relationship with our body if we are experiencing failure or frustration with the way it appears to have let us down?*

Gangloff (2024) discussed the two opposing forces between body reality and body ideal. Body ideal is a viewpoint of how we want our bodies to present to others; body reality is our body factually as it stands in life. In chronic conditions, as well as in other interrupters we are discussing in this chapter, our body's reality changes due to a disease or ongoing illness. This causes a disturbance in how we perceive our bodies and how we interact with them.

Key Terms:

Body ideal: *The viewpoint with how we want our bodies to present and look to others.*
Body reality: *The factual and actual way that our bodies present.*

It's important to distinguish the difference here between body image disturbance and body image distortion. A disturbance is an interrupter specifically because our body has changed physically, and how we relate to it has changed. Body image distortion is related to an issue of perception for how our body appears, and the issue lies with being able to see and observe our body accurately (Gangloff, 2024).

Gangloff (2024) further defined these concepts:

Body image disturbance can be a result of physical changes in the body due to a medical condition, surgery or accident. After my surgery, my body no longer felt like my own—I had 3 large scars, my hips and my ribs were in a different place and I was even standing taller. It was difficult to look in the mirror or even touch my back because I felt like a stranger. These changes in my body were uncomfortable and distressing.

There is a loss that occurs about how our bodies present, how they are when we face serious health challenges. We need time and space to be able to process this free of judgment and scrutinization.

Spotlight Story

Latanya was diagnosed with postural orthostatic tachycardia syndrome (POTS) at the age of 22. In a matter of weeks, she went from feeling vibrant and active to struggling with a racing heart rate and an inability to keep herself upright without feeling faint or dizzy. She had struggled with negative experiences of her body throughout her life, oftentimes going to the next diet or deprivation to manage negative experiences of her body. When she began experiencing symptoms of POTS, she lost the ability to return to her old safety habits of dieting and overexercising to deal with body image issues.

As we worked through these feelings in therapy, we uncovered sadness, anger, denial and a complete disruption to her experience of her body and her connection. Our work together was to first allow space for the anger and loss she was experiencing in her body. As we processed through this, she was able to validate her feelings and begin to reestablish a new relationship with her body. It took an undoing in terms of what she knew about her body and rebuilding to find out how she could care for and enjoy her body again.

As a society we have not given people ample opportunity to feel and experience the loss around a chronic condition. My friend who had a double mastectomy following a breast cancer diagnosis needed space and time to feel loss, to realign herself with her new body. Her experience of her body changed, but because we judge and scrutinize bodies, women in particular, she internalized the messages about what her body should be rather than giving herself time to experience the loss and move to a place of compassion.

Following the onset of a chronic condition, it is very hard to trust your body when you are experiencing loss in relation to it. You are faced with having to develop a new relationship in the face of major changes. We must add in the opportunity for this new relationship to develop with our bodies in the face of major changes.

> We must add in the opportunity for this new relationship to develop with our bodies in the face of major changes.

Pregnancy

For those individuals with uteruses who have birthed children, pregnancy and the postpartum period can be a very tumultuous time with one's body. There is a heightened emphasis on body size and weight. Couple that with an emphasis on how one "should" be happy and enjoying the experience, and you have a recipe for feeling more frustration and judgment with our bodies. This creates a body image disturbance. Without appropriate time and space to adjust to this new body, you can experience a disturbance in how you feel and relate to your body.

Pregnancy and the postpartum period do not have to be body image interrupters, except that our society puts so much pressure on a pregnant person's body to gain just the right amount of weight and then "bounce back" after just a few weeks.

Throughout the pregnancy experience, health care providers closely monitor weight and weight shifts. But oftentimes, individuals are told that they only have a certain amount of weight to gain to be "healthy." The typical recommendation of 25–30 lbs leaves little or no room for the pregnant person to gain any weight throughout the

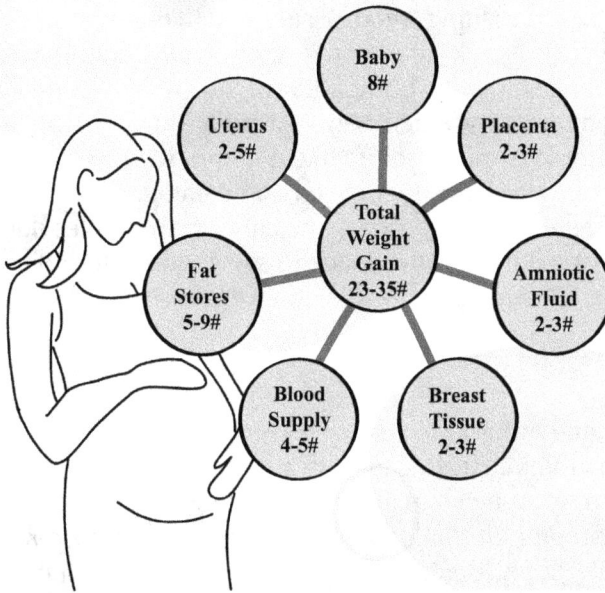

Figure 6.1 Pregnancy Weight Added Up (Kaloudis & Maio, 2024).

process aside from the fetus inside. In the image shown above, you can see that gaining only 25 lbs throughout the pregnancy process leaves no room for the individual to actually have any changes occur in their body.

During pregnancy, the body goes through many changes. After all, we are growing a human. We shouldn't place high levels of criticalness on a body that is going through so many transformations. But that is just what society does. This experience highlights again the difference between body reality and body ideal. We have an idea of what our bodies should do during pregnancy. Most times, that ideal is unrealistic based on photoshopped images and standards presented by the media.

Additionally, people in larger bodies are given an extra hard time during pregnancy, even being told that they should LOSE weight while growing a baby in their body. That is not focusing on prioritizing health but instead focusing on a one-size-fits-all philosophy that emphasizes body control versus body acceptance.

Our bodies will hormonally change during pregnancy, we will have stretch marks while our bodies grow, we will have aches and pains and hips widening. Yet diet culture will tell us that it's possible to get your "body back" after you give birth. Diet culture will tell you that the changes in your body are reversible. These messages leave us in a contradictory place between body image ideals and body image reality. We're left feeling like a failure if we can't accomplish the unrealistic standards that have been created.

We need the space to process and care for our bodies during pregnancy. What we need is the space to say goodbye to old versions of ourselves and create care for the new versions we are becoming.

Aging

The anti-aging industry is a scam.

Why do I think that? Because it's a multibillion-dollar industry designed to make us feel bad about how our bodies change in time. *As I've said throughout this book, our bodies are supposed to change in time.* We don't look the same as we looked in high school or childhood. But the anti-aging industry says differently—we should all have smooth skin, no cellulite and no wrinkles. That's the goal from major marketing materials blasted at us everywhere. Why are we, especially as women, so obsessed with staying youthful? It's an industry that has established these standards. To be clear: The standards are so very different for men.

Think about all the celebrities you've seen in the media. While aging, men get names like "silver fox." The "dad bod" trend indicates how attractive they are. Yet I recently just read yet another statement by yet another aging woman who had to defend the way her face had changed with wrinkles. Sarah Jessica Parker literally had to defend her aging appearance to the media saying "I know what I look like. I have no choice. What am I going to do about it? Stop aging?"

Aging is different from anything that I've previously listed in this chapter. If we're lucky, aging will happen to all of us. If we are given the opportunity, our bodies will shift and change over time.

This could be a body image connector—throughout the aging process, we could allow space for understanding our bodies to a greater degree. We could care for our bodies to a greater degree.

We could have a completely different experience of bodies in this process.

But we receive pressure from so many outside sources for our bodies to appear as if they are frozen in time. We are pressured to look as if our bodies are supernatural, "defying the odds of aging" (which is, in fact, a literal slogan from a product line).

Perimenopause, or the period of hormonal shifts directly preceding menopause, begins on average at 47 years old for women or those assigned female at birth (Rosser, 2022). But that is just an average; it can begin earlier in an individual's early 40s and can create a distinct shift in mood, sleep habits and weight distribution. This is occurring as the ovaries decrease egg production and estrogen. Perimenopause is the precursor to menopause, which is defined as occurring once a person's period has had complete cessation for 12 months or longer.

Key Term:

Perimenopause: *The period of hormonal shifts directly preceding menopause.*
Menopause: The time of life where the ovaries stop producing eggs and hormones and menstrual periods stop for a consecutive 12 months.

How many of you reading this book were taught about women's health and aging? How many of you felt that you learned about it in an open way from parents or doctors? Do you feel you have appropriate information being given to you? I imagine few of you feel informed about these topics, unless you have made it your mission to understand and research this process yourself. In their book *What the Fresh Hell Is This? Perimenopause, Menopause, Other Indignities and You,* Heather Corinna (2021) laments how little they knew on perimenopause, menopause or anything adjacently related to this stage of life:

I didn't know anything about perimenopause, including that I was in it, until I had already been in it for years, despite having an array of hallmark impacts: painful cystic acne, hot flashes, night sweats, anxiety, depression including a resurgence of my suicidality, menstrual changes, digestive issues, body-composition shifts, an increase in headaches and other kinds of pain, exhaustion, and some serious cognitive challenges.

(pp. 6–7)

For many of us, reading that list can be a lightbulb moment. I know it was for me. While doing research for this portion of the book, I learned much about my own body and perimenopause, none of which I had been taught from medical practitioners or in any health class. So often we're taught it is simply a loss of estrogen, but it is so much more than this. If we are given the information and provided with a deeper understanding of what is occurring in our bodies, we would be better able to connect to our bodies rather than disconnect from them.

Again, this interrupter does not have to be an interrupter. It could be a place where we are given an opportunity to process, feel and understand what is happening in our bodies. This interrupter can be a place where our connection to our own bodies can deepen because we have learned how to care for ourselves.

This interrupter can be a place where our connection can deepen because we have learned how to care for ourselves.

Do you know how many books are out there, particularly around aging women and menopause, which talk about "getting our bodies back"? Title after title indicates there is a magic cure for hormone balance, food calculations and sleeping prescriptions. I agree that we need a better understanding of how to care for ourselves during this life transition, but I disagree that it should be about "getting our bodies back." Back to what? Haven't we grown and changed, and isn't this inherently going to be a different body from here on out? It actually is a different version of our previous body! *Our body has changed.*

This phenomenon parallels almost exactly the experience of those who have given birth. Have the baby, then get your body right back to where it was before—bounce back. We are creating pressure on those who are undergoing menopause to be just the same—your body is going through "the change" as it is so ominously referred to in pop culture, but make sure that you get it right back to where it was before. This doesn't even make sense.

Where We Go from Here

We need a new language to talk about and create connections with our bodies. We need to give ourselves permission to develop a relationship around these changes, not to just avoid or attempt to control our bodies during these times.

The interrupters list I've created are not exhaustive. Perhaps while reading you were able to identify a few other experiences throughout your life where you have experienced a disruption in how you related to your body. Perhaps you can think about ways your body has changed over time and how that has affected you. Take what we are discussing in this chapter and apply that to those experiences as well.

We must both validate how we feel about these changes or other difficult experiences in our bodies and give ourselves compassion and grace as our bodies change. We give grace to children's bodies as they grow and change. We celebrate a child's body getting taller. We celebrate a young girl going through puberty. Can we care for and create a new language for ourselves?

Journal Topics

1   What does the difference between body ideal and body reality mean to you?
2   Were you taught about acceptance as your body changed or were you conditioned to fight against it?
3   How would it feel to experience acceptance and compassion for your changing body?

Only Have a Few Minutes? A Few Key Points to Focus On

1   It's important to understand that "bounce back" ideal for bodies following physical changes (surgeries, injuries, chronic conditions, pregnancy, aging) is a toxic ideal established by diet culture.

2   Instead of focusing on having our body return to what it was in the past, we must give space for healing and allow our bodies to change.

3   Chronic conditions, aging, pregnancy and the postpartum period can be interrupters if we buy into "bounce back" culture. But there is opportunity for us to allow them to be places for more communication with our body.

4   The difference between body ideal (the viewpoint with how we want our bodies to present and look to others) and body reality (the factual and actual way that our bodies present) can create body image disturbance. Our work is to reconcile and teach a new language to our bodies.

References

Agency for Healthcare Research and Quality. (n.d.). *Chronic conditions.* https://www.ahrq.gov/topics/chronic-conditions.html

Corinna, H. (2021). *What fresh hell is this? Perimenopause, menopause, other indignities and you.* Hachette.

Gangloff, T. (2024, March 23). *Chronic medical conditions, body image, eating disorders and resilience.* International Association of Eating Disorder Annual Conference, Miami, FL.

Kaloudis, A. & Maio, H. (2024, March 22). *Under pressure: Eating disorders in the perinatal period.* International Association of Eating Disorder Annual Conference, Miami, FL.

Rosser, M. (2022, June 7). *Everything you need to know about perimenopause.* Columbia University Irving Medical Center. https://www.cuimc.columbia.edu/news/everything-you-need-know-about-perimenopause

Chapter 7

Parenting and Body Image

Healing Ourselves, Healing the Future Generation

> **Myth Debunked**
>
> "Mom says I need to watch my weight."
>
> *In her book,* You're Wearing That? Understanding Mothers and Daughters in Conversation, *Deborah Tannen (2006) discusses three main topics of friction between moms and daughters: hair, clothing and weight. Mothers desire to "protect" her daughter(s). Obviously this is not true in all mother/daughter relationships, but research indicates that parents, specifically mothers, focus on these areas as a means of attempting to "save" their daughter from the heartache they themselves experienced.*
>
> *The problem is that focus on these areas increases insecurity for daughters. If you've had a mother who focused on weight loss as a means of bettering herself, you can probably identify the hurt it caused to hear these things from your parents. Being told to lose weight increases insecurity; having weight monitored from a source whom you trust inflicts worry about weight throughout your life.*
>
> *Many times, parents who express concerns around weight are reinforcing worries from their own childhood. If we experienced these types of comments from our parents, we should think about whether we believe those messages. Just because your mom or dad said it doesn't make it true.*

This chapter is for those of you who have been parented and for those of you who are parenting. It is important for us to understand the links between how we've been parented, the messages we've

DOI: 10.4324/9781032654799-9

taken in and how they have impacted us. If you grew up watching your parents' cycle through every new diet trend and obsessing about what they see in the mirror, their behaviors will trickle down to your own beliefs and behaviors. It will become a brick in your wall. There is no getting around that. We need a little (or a lot) of rebellion in finding peace with our bodies. Rebellion involves undoing and unraveling the messages our parents may have given us about our bodies and rebuilding to be strong and connective.

For those who are parents, there is a great responsibility to not inadvertently pass on the negative messaging we received from past generations. I've already told you about my experience with hearing my grandmother express hatred with her body. It affected me; it was a brick in my wall. I learned how to engage with my body by hearing those I trusted talk about their own self-hatred. As parents, we hold a responsibility to change the dialogue around bodies and body image for our children.

I need to make one thing clear: I do not blame a single person stuck in this chronic dieting and chronic body-hatred generational cycle. I don't blame the grandmother or the great-grandmother or the mother. I am not judging or criticizing you as a parent if you have unknowingly or inadvertently used language with your children that could be impacting their body image. I don't blame or judge someone who, without realizing their effect, helped their child diet to work on body image issues. I would never judge a person who decided to use a weight loss injection to heal the years of body shaming they experienced. However, I do judge a society that is fixated on thinness. I judge an industry that makes money from women's self-hatred.

We may learn from our family lineage to feel shame about bodies, and then we end up passing that shame on to our children. Until we know better, we can't do better. But once we know, it's our time to change the tide and create change. Let's do that now.

Correlation between Body Shame and Generational Chronic Dieting

There is ample evidence about the impact of having chronic dieting parents and a child's own eating patterns. A literature review of the above topics conducted in 2023 produced the following results:

> According to the findings, teenagers who had a family member who was dieting were more likely to have disordered eating

attitudes than those who did not. It was hypothesized that the presence of a dieting family member may signal greater concerns about eating, dieting and body image in adolescents.

(Kontele et al., 2023)

We learn how to interact with our bodies and ourselves from our parents and our family line. As we've talked about earlier, genetics loads the gun, but these messages can pull the trigger.

In my own clinical practice, throughout my years of practicing and specializing in body image concerns and eating disorder needs, I can only think of a few clients who did not tell me about their mother or father expressing body image self-hatred. Almost all of the clients that I've seen who have expressed body hatred can recount stories of one of their parents (or in some cases both of their parents) expressing hatred about their own bodies. Read that again and let it sink in. We are directly impacted by how bodies are talked about and taken care of in our families.

We are directly impacted by how bodies are talked about and taken care of in our families.

Spotlight Story

Terri is a 35-year-old woman who struggled with body image issues her entire life. When discussing her own body image history, she has clear memories of being a young child and watching her mother use a tape measure to gauge the circumference of her thighs or stomach. Bookshelves in her house growing up were filled with books on the latest fad diet—Jenny Craig, SlimFast, Atkins and the list goes on. At age 12, she was taken to her first Weight Watchers meeting with her mom to learn how to use points. She was told from a young age that thinner is better, that nothing tastes as good as skinny feels and that she would not secure a relationship if her body was too large. She can't remember a time where her mother sat down and ate the same meal as the family. Instead, Terri remembered her mom would typically cook a separate meal for herself that fit her latest diet needs. At the age of 15, Terri began eating the diet meals with her mother instead of the other meals that were made for the rest of the family. She weighed herself morning and night with the scale that was readily available in the bathroom. She tracked the numbers religiously, just like her mother taught her to do.

When Terri came into therapy to work on her self-hatred with her body, she brought with her years of memories of being taught that she had to control her mind and her body, leaving her yo-yo dieting for 20-plus years. With each diet she would drop a significant amount of weight, leaving her feeling elated and on top of the world. She would receive praise from her mother about how beautiful and desirable she was to others. Inevitably, the diet would fail, and she would gain the weight back and then some. Every time this cycle happened, Terri's mother would offer to go back on a diet with her, to try the next miracle cure. The latest intervention Terri and her mother did together was the Ozempic injection. This was a final straw for Terri as she became increasingly nauseous, with severe GI responses.

Through therapy, Terri began to realize that the messaging she had received from her mother came from her mother's own brokenness. Terri had grown up thinking that she had to change her body to like her body and that the only way to do this was through a new diet. Her mother had inadvertently passed on body self-hatred in the name of bettering her daughter's body.

The False Association of "Health" with Body Size in Children

"But I just want my kid to be healthy." This is a phrase I hear so often among clients and friends and across social media. Of course we want our kids to be healthy! No one among us says, "Oh I wish my kid would struggle with a major health crisis." The problem is that to create and emphasize health in our children, more often than not we inadvertently drop seeds of shame.

The problem is that in an effort to create and emphasize health in our children, more often than not we are inadvertently dropping seeds of shame.

Think back to our discussion of the diet industry and its major impact on how we view bodies and health. We outlined specifically how weight emphasis impacts body image. We discussed how weight cannot be our sole indicator of health. Unfortunately, too often we overemphasize weights and numbers with our children to their own detriment. Perhaps we experienced this ourselves as children too.

Children Perceive Their Bodies According to Their Family's Body Talk

Our children learn about what is healthy or unhealthy for them based specifically on the messages parents give. How our children learn to interact with the messages from the outside world is based on how parents teach them to respond and feel.

- So how do we raise healthy kids rather than kids purely obsessed with and fixated on numbers and diets?
- How do we raise children who know and experience the value of their bodies rather than overemphasizing control and the need to shift their bodies?

Reflect on your own experiences with your parents and what you learned throughout your life:

- Were you raised in an environment where you were taught to value and appreciate your body?
- Did you hear the adults around you expressing compassion and care for their bodies?
- Did you learn about your body and how it works?

If you can answer "no" to any of these questions, I want you to think about a reparenting of yourself while we discuss the next set of parenting interventions. The child in you needs to be taught how to value and care for their body. If you lacked that as a child, it's never too late to give that to yourself again. Even as an adult, you can provide just that kind of parenting for yourself now. So even if you are not currently parenting children, as you read the next several sections, think about how you could parent yourself in this way.

And if you are parenting children, think about how you may want to parent them around body and body image in a different way from what you were taught. We do not have to keep up the negative body image patterns that were passed down to us from generation to generation. We can create changes for ourselves and for the future generations.

We do not have to keep up the negative body image patterns that were passed down to us from generation to generation.

Key Behaviors for Helping Our Kids with Body Image

What are safety techniques we can utilize to ensure that our kids are growing up with a strong sense of their body and body positivity? Reading this book is a start! Healing your own relationship with your body and body image is an important step. And from that, we can answer and guide them in a manner that is conducive to connectivity for their bodies rather than disconnection. We're learning this directly for ourselves but teaching it to our kids as well.

Safety Tip #1: Stop Focusing on Weight

We already discussed this earlier when we were dismantling diet systems in our life. It's very important for our children that we move away from number-focused patterns. Get rid of your scale. Get rid of it for yourself and for your children.

In her book, *Fat Talk: Parenting in the Age of Diet* Culture, Virginia Sole-Smith (2023) outlines directly what we should know when dealing with fat bias and our children. "When we teach our kids that their bodies need to be small to be good, we are also teaching them that their bodies need to be controlled" (p. xxvi). Think about your own history with body image messages you received. Chances are you will see and uncover messages that taught you to control your body rather than care for it.

Get rid of the focus on weights, get rid of the focus on numbers. Sole-Smith (2023) goes on to say,

> This is not what we want any of our kids growing up knowing. But we can't edit or rewrite every cultural message our children get about gender roles and control . . . instead we must teach them to reject these messages—even when they hear them from us.
>
> (p. xxvi)

Here's the bottom line: Move away from numbers and focus specifically on care for bodies.

Typically, when I talk about this, people will ask, "But what if my kid needs to gain weight?" or "What if my kid is not healthy?" Again, I understand the emphasis on wanting our kids to be healthy, but we need a new language for this. We need to redefine what health is for ourselves and for our kids. And the key is moving away from numbers and toward connection between their mind and body. The focus is building a strong relationship between the two. That is the health we need to focus on for everyone in our family.

Safety Tip #2: Teach Your Kids Clearly about How Bodies Work, How Specifically Their Own Body Functions and the Appropriate Names for Body Parts

Let's return to one of our earlier discussions (in Chapter 6) on one of our own body image connection interrupters—aging. One of the key points that is important for us to feel connected rather than disconnected through the menopause and perimenopause process is to understand what is happening with our bodies.

For our children it is the same thing; they need to understand how their body works, how it functions and how to care for it. It is imperative that they know the appropriate names for their body parts to know how to connect to and care for their bodies.

Spotlight Story

Tiffany struggled with disconnection and negativity with her body throughout her whole life. As we worked together in therapy, we discussed the numerous ways she had learned disconnection with her body. As we completed a history of messages she had heard about her body, she recalled never hearing information regarding body parts. The language that was used around genitalia was always coded—"fanny" or "parts."

She explored the shame she felt about her body, about its parts and about how it functioned. She recalled moments of masturbation and the deep shame that she felt when touching her own body.

Now into adulthood, Tiffany carried with her the shame she internalized around her body. She struggled with connection during sex with her partner; she felt shame related to her body and how it functioned. That shame created a disconnection between how to care for and connect to her body. Our work together was to undo the negative messages she had received about her body and its desires as well as to help her release shame by educating herself around her body, how it works and what it needs.

If you find yourself relating to any of the things described in my client Tiffany's story, a very healing step could be to reparent yourself through understanding your physical body and its needs. Educate, care for and learn how to take care of your body. Do the same for your children. Education and understanding decrease shame.

Safety Tip #3: Watch What You Say about Good and Bad Related to Food or Bodies

My three kids have commented on how my body changes time and time again, such as "Mom, your thighs are getting bigger and wigglier. They weren't always that wiggly!" I answer them with "Yep! Bodies change in time."

Obviously, I've been able to come to this type of answer after do-ing years of body image recovery work. I wouldn't have been able to answer my kids with such neutrality about my own thighs if I hadn't worked on compassion and care for my body throughout time. So again, kudos to you for picking up this book and working on your body image so you can talk about these things from a much more neutral place.

Moving away from good and bad dialogues about bodies is so key in helping our kids with body image.

- What would your relationship with your body look like if you learned that bodies were allowed to change instead of watching your parents criticize certain foods and criticize certain bodies?
- What would your relationship with your body look like if you were given a free and open language to discuss food freedom and intuition?

There is a danger in speaking dichotomously about bodies. Specifi-cally, because bodies change through time, even if our children are meeting the thin standards set forth by our media or diet industry at one time, chances are that throughout their lives that may shift. Think about Chapter 6 on body image interrupters—chronic condi-tions, pregnancy and aging. Our bodies will change. If in our forma-tive years, we learn that we should fit into a certain box in order for our bodies to be good, we are subject to feeling more negative about ourselves when our bodies almost inevitably leave that box.

We need to be clear with our children that not one body type is better or worse than another. Move away from these binary dis-cussions. Talk about body image in a more neutral way, not setting up unrealistic standards around sizes and growth charts. This helps our children feel connected and stabilized in their body image experience.

Safety Tip #4: Elevate and Encourage Body Diversity

Our children are paying attention to what we say about bodies. They're listening to how we speak about others' bodies. They're listening to what we say about our own bodies. It's so very impor-tant that we give them a language for how different each person's body is.

One thing that I say time and time again to my clients and to my children is that if we all ate the same thing and moved the same way, everyone's bodies would still look different. Bodies come in all shapes and sizes. Bodies move in all different ways. When I say this, most people agree.

Bodies come in all shapes and sizes. Bodies move in all different ways.

But here's where things can get a little more controversial—thinner bodies exist for some people naturally, but so do larger bodies. There are individuals who will naturally be in larger bodies, in fat bodies, and that is a beautiful part of body diversity. We need to give a language to our children to understand that. When your kid says, "Oh, I feel fat" or "that person is fat," we need not shy away from that but discuss more openly that fat bodies are OK.

If you're appalled or fearful regarding your child being in a fatter body, I ask you to think through what that means about your own fears with being in a larger body and why you are afraid of this. Chances are, you'll find yourself back in memories that directly relate to the messaging you received as a child about bodies. We can change the patterns for ourselves and for our children.

Journal Topics

1   How were you parented regarding bodies? What messages did you take in?
2   How do these messages still impact your body image now?
3   If you are currently a parent, is how you are discussing bodies dichotomous? Are there ways you could become more neutral in how you think and teach about bodies to your children?

Only Have a Few Minutes? A Few Key Points to Focus On

1   The generational component of body image is well researched and understood. As children, we all learned language for caring for our bodies, body ideals and body types.

2   Because of this inherited component, we need to be careful about the language and messages we send to our children regarding bodies and food.

3   Four safety techniques help us to communicate clearly and directly and without harm:

    A   Stop focusing on weight.
    B   Teach children about how bodies work and function as well as appropriate anatomy.
    C   Decrease the language related to good/bad food and bodies.
    D   Elevate and encourage body diversity.

4   It is important that we understand that we build our children up in language and connection throughout their lives.

References

Kontele, I., Saripanagiotou, S., Papadopoulou, A., Zoumbaneas, E., & Vassilakou, T. (2023). Parental dieting and correlation with disordered eating behaviours in adolescents: A narrative review. *Adolescents*, *3*(3), 538–549. https://doi.org/10.3390/adolescents3030038

Sole-Smith, V. (2023). *Fat talk: Parenting in the age of diet culture*. Henry Holt & Company.

Tannen, D. (2006). *You're wearing that? Understanding mothers and daughters in conversation*. Random House.

Part 2

A Healing of Our Past and Present Parts

Chapter 8

Changing the Messaging

Myth Debunked

"The injection will fix my relationship with my body."

The market is filled with weight loss injection drugs, which promise weight loss and solutions to the "obesity epidemic" in the world. These injection shots mimic a hormone called glucagon-like peptide-1 (GLP-1) that targets areas of the brain that regulate appetite and food intake (Office of the Commissioner, 2021). Yes, in many situations, these injections will assist in weight loss. But no, losing weight will not fix your relationship with your body.

When we think about changing our relationship with our body image simply as changing our body, we miss a huge underlying component to what actually creates this relationship: our history with the media and culture, our family and genetics and our own mental health experiences. An injection is not going to fix those memories. Changing our body is not going to change our experiences from the past with our body image. Changing our body is not going to fix a history of negativity with our thighs or our stomach. Instead, we need a complete overhaul of memories, beliefs and ideas of how we connect to our bodies and ourselves. Weight and weight loss are irrelevant to all of this.

We've examined why we've developed negative belief systems with our bodies. Until now, we've been looking at things from a macro level—or the social and cultural components that have built up our

DOI: 10.4324/9781032654799-11

body image beliefs. Now it's time to zoom in and begin the shift in our own personal beliefs about ourselves. That's why you're here, right? To create a shift in how YOU feel about your body.

You heard my story. I had so many realizations when I was given a lens for understanding how my self-hatred was birthed from a society that taught women to feel discontent with their bodies. Anne Lamott, India Arie and Jean Kilbourne—these authors and artists helped me understand the social and cultural issues at play regarding women's bodies.

The first step for me was to rebel against the systems that had taught me that my body wasn't good enough. Simple frustration wasn't enough, and I needed to build tools and skills to reinforce a positive connection with my body.

The next steps for healing my body image required me to step deeper into my own personal thought patterns and create a real shift. For that, I needed to understand and face why I struggled to tolerate my body and why I felt it needed to be fixed.

This is where the second half of this book goes. This will be where we dive into our own mental health needs, our own thought systems and our family and inherited thought patterns. Here we are creating a toolbox for managing intense feelings and changing belief systems.

To shift our beliefs about our bodies, each chapter going forward will have emotion regulation and distress tolerance tools to shift these old patterns. In addition to this, the chapters will have a few mantras, five in total, which will guide you in changing your relationship with your body.

Here's our first mantra: *This shift starts with gentleness.* That is our core basic framework for shifting this litany of negative voices in our life. Everything we do to shift our body image flows from gentleness.

A key to developing this gentleness is to understand that we deserve to take up space. It can be hard to believe this when our minds are filled with feelings and thoughts that just repeat the negative. This is understandable when all the ads we see tell us otherwise about our bodies. We learn, from history and from current messages in the media that women's bodies should fit perfectly in the box that they are assigned. Let's ditch this view once and for all.

This book will help you shift your own thoughts to believe that you and your body are allowed to take up as much space as you need. And here's a reminder: Negative thoughts that tell you to shrink yourself are built off of repetition. They become like a wall, brick by brick laid throughout time. We don't come from this wall to complete love immediately. That is why we first start with gentleness and compassion.

Embrace Gentleness and Compassion to Create Change

One of the most important things we can do is to admit the impact of the dominant culture on our belief systems about ourselves. We've spent time discussing this in past chapters because the impact from the culture is so strong. When we realize that impact, we're able to understand even further why it is so important to give ourselves kindness. It is an uphill battle, one that sometimes feels like it doesn't end. But I promise it does. Stick with it.

So here we start our journey toward freedom, and it begins with gentleness in our own minds. Does that sound too simple? Well, yes in some ways it is. But anyone who has lived in their own mind for a few minutes can tell you that gentleness is oftentimes not our modus operandi.

Dr. Kristin Neff speaks and writes on the topics of self-esteem and the ways we grow self-compassion for ourselves. When I think about our first mantra, *starting with gentleness*, I am reminded of one of Neff's (2024) writings on self-compassion:

> Instead of mercilessly judging and criticizing yourself for various inadequacies or shortcomings, self-compassion means you are kind and understanding when confronted with personal failings— after all, who ever said you were supposed to be perfect?

We cannot embark on this process without creating and practicing self-compassion. The process of shifting your relationship with your body will have a lot of ups and downs, twists and turns, and you will need self-compassion in order to give yourself grace and care through it.

There is a parallel here for belief systems about your body. Your body deserves self-compassion. Your body is not perfect, and Neff's words ring true here—after all, who ever said you were supposed to be perfect?

Let's return to our analogy of the bricks being built into a ginormous wall around us. Each brick represents a different negative thought or a different negative memory. As we've said before, these negative memories and thoughts are the basic components to our poor body image. We can't completely undo the past impact from these memories; we can't simply forget that we were told these things or that they shaped our past thinking. But what we can do is travel back to the memory and sprinkle gentleness, self-compassion and kindness into them.

Reframing My Own Childhood Memory

Let's take my example from childhood: My weight was higher than my friend's weight as a second grader. I will ask a few questions to reframe this memory.

1 What does it look like if I remove the shame from that context and just let it be?
2 What does it look like to have gentleness and self-compassion at the forefront of this memory?

When I look at the memory with these questions in mind, here's what emerges:

1 My weight was higher. Period. I don't need follow-up statements or rejection from accepting.
2 Through a lens of compassion, the whole narrative of the memory changes. I can look at it with the element of shame removed, maybe even enjoying the parts of myself that were unique. It takes the whole script of what we've been taught as women from a young age and flips it on its head.

What are we really looking for when we're seeking betterment with our bodies? We want a very specific way to feel secure about ourselves. We've been conditioned to believe that this comes from chiseled abs or weight loss on a scale. I can guarantee you'll never find enough security from a number on a scale; it will not give you what you ultimately are searching for. This is why gentleness and self-compassion are so important at the beginning of this healing journey. Because what we're doing is rebuilding self-esteem; we are learning how to give ourselves something that we were lacking or that got taken away from us earlier in our lives. We are creating a new way to look at our bodies. Belief systems with compassion at the core are the keys to moving beyond body hatred. It all ties back to believing that we deserve to take up space.

It all ties back to believing that we deserve to take up space.

Identifying What We Need and Deserve

We have been conditioned to believe that we are supposed to be smaller to be better, that we must fit a mold. It's about perfection rather than acceptance. But security doesn't come from this. Security starts from a deeper understanding of what we deserve and builds from there. We are working to switch the way we talk to ourselves, to build compassion and gentleness. And yes, you deserve that.

In small and big ways, women are told that they don't matter much and that their value comes more from the size of their body than from the work we do in this the world. Another example is this. Think about the disparity in income that we see between women and men; even this can be related back to body image issues. In a recent *Forbes* article outlining the divisions among pay among men, women and BIPOC communities, the following statistics were reported: Women earn 16% less than men on average. White women earn just 84 cents for every dollar a man makes. Women of color are among the lowest-paid workers in rural areas, with rural Black and Hispanic women making just 56 cents for every dollar that rural white, non-Hispanic men make (Haan, 2024). These are staggering differences.

As women, we are told that our work is not as valuable as what our male counterparts produce. We are told that our value comes from how we *present* versus who we are. We are told that we should be grateful for what we are given and not take up too much space. That all relates back to body image and how we think of our bodies in these moments.

Tool 1: Shade the Memory

- How do we create a shift?
- How do we not continue to get stuck in cycles of looking to our bodies to define our value?

In this chapter, we have two specific tools we can use to shift our thoughts from negative to compassionate. The first tool I'm calling *shade the memory*.

Let's look back at some of the memories and bricks we outlined in our earlier homework from Chapter 2. Look at the messages that are critical, judgmental and shaming. Next, note what specific feelings or thoughts you have about these memories and messages—label them with an honest answer about how you feel about yourself and your body when you remember them.

Here is a list of feeling words, but please do not feel limited by this. It's a starting-off point if you're struggling to find the right words to identify your feelings.

Shame	Hurt
Embarrassment	Despair
Sad	Frustration
Anger	Fear

We're going to begin moving these bricks. Some of them may feel impossible to shift. I know, I get it. Some have some very deep hurts, and some create pain even just to look at them. But little by little, with our mantra of *it all starts with gentleness*, let's shift those bricks. I promise, it is possible.

Let's try to *shade the memory*. You've labeled the hurtful messaging that you have internalized throughout the years. Now we work to shift the messages you've internalized.

Take the feelings you've labeled, and we're going to shade them through the lens of compassion. How do we do this? We pair the negative feeling with a compassionate response. If this is difficult to do because of anger or shame, think about how to externalize the memory or thought as if this was a close friend of yours who experienced this. Perhaps, it may be easy to shade the memory with compassion for your childhood self. In my recovery journey, I did this often. I would have to pause and ask, "What would compassion for little Johanna look like?"

Utilize one of these externalization frames to make it easier to express an alternative point of view than your own negative voice.

We take these negative feelings and we then pair it with gentleness. If you're having trouble accessing an emotional language for this, I am including a list of compassionate language terms to use for yourself. Sit with them for a minute and think about what might actually be able to shade your memory in a different way.

Acceptance	Care
Love	Pride
Hope	Defensiveness
Resiliency	Grace

Here's an example from my not-so-distant past. Remember the woman who told me how beautiful I "could" be if I just fixed my posture? When I first experienced that, even as a grown adult, I felt embarrassment and shame. If I were completing this exercise with that memory, I would first assign it the feeling of embarrassment. But then I need to move into the next step of looking at that experience with compassion.

Here I look at myself in this memory from a lens of compassion. Because this judgment occurred to me as an adult, it was hard for me to shift to compassion right away. This is where externalizing it as if it were an interaction that happened to a close friend was helpful. What would I say or what words of compassion would I give to a friend if they were told something so critical? This is an easier task for me to complete. I can give them grace, I can give their posture forgiveness and actually even think of friends without perfect postures who I see as beautiful in so many ways. Now I've shaded my memory from embarrassment, and I am able to view it with grace, perhaps some defensiveness, some rebellion. I see beauty in imperfection.

This is no easy task; I've worked on this process for years. So again, let's review what we talked about in earlier chapters. This wall, these memories of embarrassment and shame, were laid brick by brick over the years. It will take time and care and intentionality to undo it. We must go back to our first tip of it all starting with gentleness. But brick by brick, we can shade our memories in a different way.

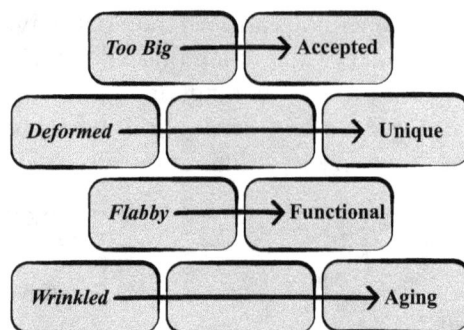

Figure 8.1 Shading Our Memories Brick by Brick.

Tool 2: Change the Script

The second tool we use to grow our compassion voice is *change the script*. I want you to pause and think about some of the celebrity icons who speak about self-love and compassion for their bodies—Lizzo comes to mind first for me. She's incredibly vocal about her love and appreciation for her body. But she's also indicated that she didn't always think this way. She hasn't openly discussed her process for shifting her beliefs about her body, but I am willing to bet it started with shifting compassion in both memories and critical voices. We are *changing the script* for ourselves and for our memories.

Spotlight Story

Sharon is a 40-year-old woman who first came to see me in the throws of struggling with severe negative thoughts about her body. She was using all the different diet culture tactics to feel better about herself—extreme diets, cleanses and workouts. Her whole focus was on the idea that if she changed her body, kept her diet just right and burned this many calories in a day, then she would feel better and see her body in a better light.

Together we worked extensively to poke holes in all the different diet culture messages that she'd internalized.

We talked extensively about things like the parietal cortex and how an undernourished body has even more difficulty seeing itself clearly. One day she walked into my office and admitted, "I just can't keep this up anymore, the constant diets and onslaught of negative experiences, the self-hatred."

Surrendering and letting go of the lies that diet culture had told her was her first step. Next we worked on changing the thoughts that had held her captive for so long. We looked at all the areas of body image that had impacted her beliefs—her own mental health, her cultural norms and her family. We used these areas to think clearly about her own memories, her "bricks" in the wall.

One specific memory stuck out to her where her father had told her a specific weight that she thought would be the "best" place for Sharon to maintain. Up until this point in our work, Sharon was still trying to maintain that number on the scale—a number that was given to her in her teenage years by a parent who was also infected by diet culture. We went back to that memory, and we gave it a lens of compassion for her as a child replacing it with messages she needed to hear about her body at the time. We let go of the numbers, and with that, shifted the experience of what her body "should" be. And we allowed gentleness and compassion to guide her further.

There is a type of therapy—Cognitive Behavioral Therapy (CBT) that emphasizes how our cognitions (thoughts) effect feelings, which in turn effect behaviors. The formula we often see for this is:

Thoughts + Feelings = Behaviors

Think about it this way: If I think about my thighs negatively with words like "too big" or "jiggly" or "filled with cellulite," these thoughts will impact my feelings about my thighs. I in turn feel shame, anger or sadness about my thighs. And next, I shrink away from wearing shorts or putting on a bathing suit. This behavior reinforces the negative voices that have already filled my head. Now I believe that my thighs don't deserve to be shown, and because I don't put on the bathing suit, I never have any feedback for myself that opposes this. The cycle continues and I am left feeling hopeless about my body.

So where do we start to shift this cycle? In this chapter, we start with building a compassionate voice in our head to shift the thoughts. In future chapters, we'll talk more about creating a shift first in behaviors, but that comes later. For now, we shift the thoughts by creating a new, compassionate voice in our thoughts.

The first step is to begin to recognize that these voices are critical and negative and unnecessary. This is why we first had to talk about the cultural context of body image ideals and diet culture. Diet culture will tell us that our critical voices make us better. That they force us to change. I say that they make us feel worse, behave worse and have no place in our mind. The key is gentleness.

I want to be very, very clear here: We cannot shift negative body image simply by shifting our thoughts about our body. This is because body image, our experience of our bodies, is so much more than simply something that is made up just of our thoughts. But we are starting with our thoughts as an entry point, as a way of stepping out of the endless cycle of shaming ourselves, shaming our bodies and then hiding away from experiences and enjoyment that might help create the shift as well.

We begin with shifting the way we talk to our bodies, the way we relate to our bodies. From there, we make more changes related to being in and connected to our bodies. More than anything else, a shift in thoughts helps us jump into those umbrellas we discussed that make up our body image—our cultural and societal messages, our family and genetic messages and our own mental health needs. We start with thoughts and move to all the other experiential components.

Look back at the journal prompts at the end of Chapter 3 where we discuss the negative messaging that's impacting your thoughts. I asked you to list negative thoughts about your body throughout a day. Let's take those thoughts and with a lens of compassion utilize the *change the script tool*. We build a new voice in this way. First, we have our list of negative statements we have placed upon our bodies over the course of a day (whew, I know it can be hard to see all of those statements in one place!). But don't worry, we will work on compassionately shifting these thoughts.

Reframe the Way We See the World

We need a direct understanding of the role of distorted thinking in these tainted thoughts. Think of a distortion, or more specifically a cognitive distortion, as this: an unhelping way of seeing or experiencing the world. "Cognitive distortions involve negative thinking patterns that aren't based on fact or reality" (Stanborough, 2022).

Below is a list of types of distortions adapted from David Burns's *The Feeling Good Handbook* (1999). Read over them carefully. This is not an exhaustive list of distortions but is instead my handpicked list that I've seen impact my clients' body image belief systems. Think about ways in which your body image thoughts may have a lens of distortion to them.

Key Term:

Cognitive distortion: *A negative thought pattern that is not based on fact or reality. An unhelpful way of seeing or experiencing the world.*

Cognitive Distortions List

- *All-or-nothing thinking:* You see things in black or white categories. If a situation or your body falls short of perfect, you see it as a total failure.
- *Over generalization:* You see a single negative event, such as a romantic rejection or a negative comment about your body, as a never-ending pattern by using words such as "always" or "never" when you think about it.
- *Mental filter:* You pick out a single negative detail and dwell on it exclusively so that your vision of all reality becomes darkened.

- *Discounting the positive:* You reject positive experiences by insisting they "don't count." If you receive a compliment, you may discount it or excuse it away.
- *Magnification:* You exaggerate the importance of your problems and shortcomings, or areas of your body, that you don't like, and you minimize the importance of your desirable qualities. This is also called the "binocular trick."
- *Emotional reasoning:* You assume that your negative emotions necessarily reflect the way things really are: "I feel horrible about my stomach. It must be because my stomach is bad." Or "I feel guilty. I must be a rotten person."
- *"Should" statements:* You tell yourself that things "should" be the way you hoped or expected them to be. After looking in the mirror, you say to yourself, "I should be smaller." This in turn makes you feel more angry and disgusted with your body. "Musts," "oughts" and "have tos" are similar offenders.
- *Labeling*: Labeling is an extreme form of all-or-nothing thinking. Instead of saying "I have fat on my body," you attach a negative label to yourself: "I'm disgusting." These labels are just useless abstractions that lead to anger, anxiety, frustration and low self-esteem.

Shift the Thoughts

Now that we've reviewed the eight typical thought distortions that we attach to our bodies, it's time to work on shifting the thoughts. Again, remember we're doing this all under a lens of compassion. I am not asking you to spew positivity at these thoughts—"I love my thighs!" What I've found to be impossible, bordering on toxic positivity, is to try to shift the thoughts by moving to their extreme counterparts. What I mean by that is to try to take a thought such as "I have gross thighs" and shift it directly to "I have perfect thighs." The critical thoughts are so ingrained, it's impossible to just shift them to the other extreme. You wouldn't even believe it! And what good does that do? And what are "perfect" thighs anyways?

When we label a distortion within our thoughts, first and foremost, it helps us shift just a little bit. And what does that shift look like?

Let's take my earlier example: "I have gross thighs." Let's first identify a distortion at play in this thought process. Any number of these
distortions listed above would fit, but for right now, let's choose "labeling." How is this labeling? Because you have attached a specific,
negative label to your thighs. Instead of saying, "My thighs have fat"
and staying in neutrality, you've labeled them as something negative
and in turn fueled anger toward your thighs.

• What would it look like to balance that thought?
• What would it look like to shift it just a little for it to lose its power
  over you?

To go back to our focus of this chapter, it's all about compassion
in your approach. We identify the negative thought, we label the
distortion at play with it and then we put compassion as a covering
over it all.

How do I engage with the thought "My thighs are gross" when
I've put the lens of compassion on them? The first step in a compassionate response is to think about the ways your thighs function for
you—they hold you up, they move your body and they connect your
torso to your knees and calves. Shift your thinking from self-hatred
thoughts, "My thighs are gross," to "Here are how my thighs function for me."

We are starting with functionality and neutrality to balance our
negative thoughts. I believe we can go further than just changing
our thoughts from negative to impartial description. However, this
neutrality lays a groundwork for us to begin reconnection and communication with our bodies. We start here, but we don't stay here.
Stay tuned for future chapters to take us further into connection and
care.

For now, starting with a compassionate gentleness for our bodies
means that we can move from how our body parts function into a
lens of neutrality. I'm including a version of a CBT thought log for us
to practice this. This is in no means a traditional CBT thought log, it's
my own body image worksheet for use as a way of managing these
thoughts. The first line that I'm showing is an example from my own
work with my body image, one where I've been able to shift my enjoyment of my body in specific ways.

Critical Body Thought	Type of Distortion	Functional Component to Body	Neutralizing Compassionate Thought
My stomach is too big.	All-or-nothing thinking	My stomach holds my organs, it holds my body up. It has fat, which protects the vital organs I have.	My stomach is not perfect, but I can practice compassion and gratefulness for all it does for me.

Notice in the last column, I didn't shift my thoughts to "I love my stomach" or "My stomach is perfect"—that's not our goal right now. The goal is shifting the internalized dialogue about our stomachs. And when we shift our thoughts, we shift our feelings and behaviors.

It takes time; by no means do I think that you read this book, fill out this column and then feel amazing about all body parts. But I promise that if you shift the thoughts initially to neutrality, then you will slowly be able to shift the thoughts to the point of feeling some relief. It will slowly create a whole different belief system about your own body. But remember our second chapter; it takes time.

To review, in this chapter we outlined how extensively important compassion is for the root of changing body image belief systems. We cannot change our relationship with our bodies without changing how we interact with ourselves. Practicing compassion and gentleness is the first step, and the only first step, to changing our belief system about ourselves.

Practicing compassion and gentleness is the first step, and the only first step, to changing our belief system about ourselves.

We then outlined two tools we can use both from past memories, or bricks in the wall in front of us, as well as with our present thoughts. Our first tool is *shade the memory*. We're unlearning our negative associations with these memories, reshaping what we believe about our bodies then and now by giving a shade of compassion and a tone of grace to ourselves.

Our second tool is to *change the script*. We're working here with our present thoughts, those automatic belief systems that pop into our head when we look down at our bodies or catch a glance of ourselves in the mirror. These are pretty intense stuck points, but I promise that if we begin to shift our thoughts from the distorted to the neutral, we can create a huge change in how we feel about ourselves.

Stop for a bit and ask: What's the typical pattern with a bad body image day or a bad body image moment? It's likely that we're looking at numbers or diets or cool sculpting to work on "bettering" ourselves, making it so that our pictures or what we see in the mirror is presentable. This doesn't work; it doesn't make us feel better. This has not worked and will not work. To go back to numbers, to diets and so forth is only continuing the pattern of placing the emphasis on an external outlook rather than an internal one for security. We play back into the historical narrative that a woman's body is her primary importance. That's why looking at the history and culture around body image is so key to healing from the negativity.

- What do we do instead?
- How do we step outside of the same patterns that don't work?

Right now, we start with these two first tools to shift our thoughts. Once I was at an outdoor water park with my kids, splashing around in the water with them, riding the waves in the wave pool and lounging about down the lazy river. On one of the trips down the lazy river, I had a thought—how many times have we as women missed out on the joy in these experiences because we're thinking about or focused on how we look in a bathing suit?

I don't mean just the size of our thighs or the shape of our stomachs but also all of the judgments and criticalness we have been conditioned to believe about our bodies in general. It's conditioned in us from the beginning, marketed to hate and loathe parts of our body in the name of "betterment" or even "health." Getting rid of sunspots, achieving a no-wrinkles sort of effortless work. The pressure on women is all encompassing. So let's start with shifting our thoughts with compassion; it's our first and important step. This gives us the ability to be fully present in enjoyment in our lives.

Next, we move on to shifting our behaviors.

Journal Topics

1 What did it *feel* like to see the negative thoughts you wrote down listed in front of you?
2 Was it possible to view the distortion in them? Do you think there is a part of you that is stuck on still believing the negative parts of them? Why might that be?
3 Sometimes we continue to believe that the critical and judgmental voices cause us to better ourselves. Can you think about ways that these critical voices in your mind are actively harming you?
4 Are there specific distortions that are hard for you to challenge in your body image thoughts? Why do you think those particular types are difficult for you?

Only Have a Few Minutes? A Few Key Points to Focus On

1 Shifting our relationship with our bodies begins with a new language of compassion and gentleness for ourselves. Criticalness and judgmental thought patterns have been major influences of our development of negative body image. Covering ourselves and our beliefs in compassion is a central first step in undoing the negativity. This is our mantra of *it all starts with gentleness*.
2 It is important to take individual memories, particularly those that have contributed to core belief systems, and create a compassionate language for ourselves with them. We can bring healing to these memories with our first tool: *shading the memory with balance and compassion for our bodies*.
3 Another integral shift for healing poor body image is shifting and changing the thoughts we have regarding our bodies. Our second tool is called *the change the script tactic*. We are able to shift our thought patterns about our bodies by recognizing harmful thought patterns and balancing with a sense of neutrality. Body neutrality gives us a language for viewing our body through its functions and a non-judgmental framework.

References

Burns, D. (1999). *Feeling good: The new mood therapy*. Harper-Collins.
Haan, K. (2024, March 1). Gender pay gap statistics in 2024. *Forbes Advisor*. https://www.forbes.com/advisor/business/gender-pay-gap-statistics/#sources_section

Neff, K. (2024, April 10). *Exploring the meaning of self-compassion and its importance.* https://self-compassion.org/the-three-elements-of-self-compassion-2/

Office of the Commissioner. (2021, June 4). *FDA approves new drug treatment for chronic weight management, first since 2014.* U.S. Food and Drug Administration. https://www.fda.gov/news-events/press-announcements/fda-approves-new-drug-treatment-chronic-weight-management-first-2014

Stanborough, R. J. (2022, October 25). What are cognitive distortions and how can you change these thinking patterns? *Healthline.* https://www.healthline.com/health/cognitive-distortions#:~:text=Cognitive%20distortions%20involve%20negative%20thinking,just%20failed%20that%20math%20test.

Chapter 9

Radical Acceptance

Myth Debunked

"What I see in the mirror is exactly what I am."

Objects in the mirror are not as they appear, even though we may be 1,000% positive that we can see ourselves correctly. We need to keep in mind that there are a multitude of issues that impact what we see when we look at ourselves.

Years ago, Dove did a powerful campaign related to this. The company had portrait artists ready to draw a subject sight unseen. The subject described themselves to the artist only in words: "I have a large nose, it protrudes out," "Kind of a pear-shaped face," and so on. Dove then brought in a second individual who had previously seen the person being sketched. The second individual again described the first individual to the portrait artist. The results were startling: 100% of the time the individual who described themselves produced a much more tainted picture of themselves versus the portrait that was described by the second individual.

Yes, this is just an experiment put on by a skincare product company. But it highlights something so deep and raw. The reality is, we are our hardest and most cruel critics. This is specifically because between ourselves and the mirror, there is a layer of criticalness that we project onto our bodies. We were told we needed clear skin as a teenager and then throughout our life any pimple or blemish becomes magnified to a degree far beyond what it actually is. We project our negativity, fears,

DOI: 10.4324/9781032654799-12

> *anxieties and worst thoughts onto our bodies. We need to re-member, constantly, that what we see in the mirror is a projection of what we are feeling about ourselves in general. What we see in the mirror is NOT a direct reflection of how we actually appear.*

- What does it mean to sit with something that we can't change?
- How do we tolerate it?
- How do we stay grounded in a space when we are feeling particularly unsettled within ourselves?

A major falsehood of diet culture and the promises that the diet industry has given is that to manage the difficult feelings you may have about your body, what you have to do is change what you are struggling with in your body. In diet culture, it's not about shifting the feelings toward your body, it's all about shifting the physique of your body.

Think about it—hate how your butt looks? There's a diet for that, a workout for that and a surgery for that with implants or an injection. Here's the problem: *Changing those things about your body does not actually fix the issue you have with your body.* It may appease you for a moment, but then the unsettled feelings come back.

This happens for two reasons: The rules of what our bodies are supposed to look like are constantly changing (Big butts are in! Big butts are out! Hourglass figure is the way to go! No wait, just kidding, now it's heroin chic time!). But it also happens because at the end of the day it's not about our bodies. It's about an ingrained belief system about our bodies; it's about years of believing that we not only shouldn't like our bodies the way they are, and we absolutely shouldn't even tolerate our bodies as they are.

Practice Radical Acceptance

I propose that not only should we not be working to change our body, but also we should be radically accepting our bodies. We've tried the route of creams to rid ourselves of cellulite and extreme diets and tummy tucks to change our body shape, but none of this works. Yes, you might shift your body for a moment in time, but you won't shift your acceptance of your body. You won't shift the love for your body. That comes from a completely different approach.

Key Term:

Radical acceptance: *Complete and total openness to the facts of reality as they are, without throwing a tantrum and growing angry* (Linehan, 2022).

With these questions we come to our next tool in establishing a healthy body image—*radical acceptance*. The concept of radical acceptance comes from Marsha Linehan, the creator of dialectical behavioral therapy (DBT). She initially created DBT as a form of therapy to assist clients who were struggling with emotion regulation, and the benefits of this type of therapy are far reaching beyond any one diagnosis.

DBT has multiple modules, four specifically, that a person uses to help address difficult and tumultuous areas in an individual's life. These modules are as follows:

1   Interpersonal communication
2   Mindfulness
3   Emotion regulation
4   Distress tolerance

All of these modules work together as a therapeutic tool to help an individual tolerate and manage extreme emotions.

Analyze a Bad Body Image Moment

Jump back into those bad body image days. Head back into your memories for a moment—think about a time that your mind was filled with negativity about your body and about yourself.

• What did you do next?
• Possibly googled the next fad diet?

- Promised yourself that this time it was going to work?
- You would see it through?

I get it, I've been there. In the past, back in my most eating disordered days, I would obsessively count calories each day. I would read all the magazines telling me that if I ate under this certain amount, my stomach would flatten out, my thighs would do just what they were supposed to do and then I would feel happy.

Spoiler alert—it didn't work for me. And if you're reading this, I am guessing it didn't work for you either. Because we can't find acceptance for our body by changing our body. It's paradoxical.

We can't find acceptance for our body by changing our body. It's paradoxical.

Learn to Tolerate Distress

Here's where **radical acceptance** comes into play. Underlying radical acceptance is the belief that the agony we feel has roots related to the conflict we feel around pain. It is the resistance of the pain that causes discomfort. Because of that discomfort, we get stuck in a loop of feeling that we must change something to eradicate the pain or discomfort.

The concept of radical acceptance posits that we can shift the pain we are feeling by coming to terms with our inability to change the current situation. We cannot change the past; there may even be numerous parts of the present that we are unable to change as well. Radical acceptance essentially helps us shift our mindset from needing to change the present to working to accept the present. The suffering comes from finding it to be intolerable; the work is beginning to shift that intolerance into tolerance.

Radical acceptance is a key component of the distress tolerance module in DBT. And when you've been in the throes of a difficult and bad body image day, you know that distress is a major emotional issue at that time. It's because, in those moments, the negativity that you are feeling about your body seems insurmountable. It's distressing to really believe that your body will never be acceptable and must be changed to be better. But remember, we've disproven that there is anything wrong with your body. The problem lies in the lens we have been given to view our body. So let's first start with managing the distress, and then let's continue our work of shifting the lens.

Practice Non-Judgment

Radical acceptance gives us a tool to tolerate distress. There is a major key player here, and it's the opposite of what we've been conditioned to feel and believe. The key concept around radical acceptance that we need to practice is non-judgment. We have been conditioned from the diet industry and from diet culture to engage in judgment with our own bodies. It keeps us discontent and therefore coming back to the same industry to make us feel better.

And here is our next mantra for working through poor body image: *I can radically accept my body as it is.*

If we pull back from the judgment, pull away from the critique and look at our bodies and ourselves with a non-biased perspective, things change. Our body is our body. Period. The cellulite, the fat, the wrinkles. They exist. It's the neutrality with it that we have to develop.

"Radical acceptance does not mean that you agree with what is happening or what has happened to you. Rather, it signals a chance for hope because you are accepting things as they are and not fighting against reality" (Cuncic, 2022). I love this definition. We don't have to fight our bodies anymore. We can stay in the present, accept things as they are. It's not our bodies that are wrong; it's the struggle against our bodies that is wrong.

Coming to a place of radical acceptance is not simple. Just because we mentioned the word "radical acceptance" does not mean that the whole vantage point of how you feel about your body will change immediately. Instead, it is a practice in the letting go and the shifting. I like to use a synonym here: Acceptance is the same in many ways as receiving. I receive my body as it is. I know that sounds a little odd, and it's definitely a huge shift from what we've been taught in the environment around us. We have been given messages from our culture, from our families and/or from our own mental health struggles that tell us differently about our bodies and acceptance. But remember, so much of the heartache of poor body image is related to resistance with where our body is. Receiving where our body is, receiving it as it wants to be, that is where we find the release of judgment and the ability to radically accept.

My Own Example of Radical Acceptance and Non-Judgment

Here's an example from my own life, even something more recent than back in the old eating disordered days. I've noticed more and more wrinkles and sunspots on my skin here or there. First of all, I know that signals I need to be better about sunscreen—that's true! But it's also a signal to me that I am aging; my son was even commenting to me the other day that I have "sooooo many wrinkles." When he said this, I had a choice at that moment to resist and express anger followed by doubling down on the anti-wrinkle cream and other products. But I brought back into mind the concept of radical acceptance. I paused and thought to myself "Johanna, you can fight against aging, or you can embrace it. Radical acceptance says that wrinkles and sunspots are a part of your body. Plain and simple."

I not only stopped resisting that I am gathering wrinkles by the dozen but started radically accepting that I am getting more wrinkles. I accepted the wrinkles and by accepting, I came to a place of peace with my body. To go back to Chapter 8 where we talked about changing our thoughts, I said to myself and my wrinkles "I receive you." It created a big shift.

Tool 3: Non-Judgmental Mirror Work

Here's the third tool to start practicing to begin engaging in radical acceptance and find peace with your body. There are variations to the activity—feel free to start at whichever level feels appropriate to you. It all depends on what is the right fit for you and where your needs are.

We're calling this tool *non-judgmental mirror work*. The non-judgmental part is incredibly important. Judgment is what causes us the pain. Our work is to become observers of our bodies, not criticizers. We do this through practice, through mindfulness.

Mirror work, specifically mirror exposure work (ME; Griffen et al., 2018), as a therapeutic intervention has existed for quite some time in the eating disorder recovery field. It is a form of disengaging with the focused negativity one experiences with their own reflection. Instead, you are encouraged to take body part by body part the specific area of your person and describe in a non-judgmental way. "The power of mirrors to elicit an emotional reaction to self-viewing has been used in a variety of therapeutic modalities to treat psychiatric disorders with symptomatic negative body image" (Griffen et al., 2018). With this activity, what we are doing is working to elicit a change in our initial responses—instead of disgust or anger, we are working toward neutrality, non-judgment and radical acceptance.

Numerous studies have spoken to the efficacy and helpfulness of being able to practice neutrality and positivity while doing ME. One such study reported that there were strong indications that participating in non-judgmental ME provided relief and even connection for clients struggling with poor body image (Griffen et al., 2018).

I must note, it is advised to do this activity under the care of a therapist who is trained in eating disorder recovery work. What I am listing here is a cursory discussion of this intervention, and we are specifically keeping the discussion points at a surface level of this intervention. To go much deeper than this must be done under the direction of a professional who can act as a guide to navigate the negative thoughts that may surface.

Remember, our backdrop is non-judgment in a world that is screaming judgment at us, so this will take a fair amount of practice and compassion for yourself. If you don't shift negativity in the first go around, don't worry. Keep at it. It will shift slowly in time.

Our first step in non-judgmental mirror work is to decide what part of your body you will practice this intervention with. Start by finding a mirror. Depending on your level of negativity with your body, it can be helpful to do this one body part by body part. However, if you are in a place of tolerating more, you are welcome to start with your full body at once. If you are starting with one body part, I would begin by choosing one that is the safest or holds the least amount of negativity for you. We build our confidence with this and build up to the hardest places the more we go along.

The amount of time you spend focusing on a specific body part is also up to you. Initially, you may only be able to spend a few seconds or a minute looking at your body/body part. That's OK! Meet yourself wherever you are at. It doesn't have to be anything more than that. That's one of the most important things about this—you're relearning to be in step with your own needs, not what others are telling you to do but what instead works for you.

That's one of the most important things about this—you're re-learning to be in step with your own needs, not what others are telling you to do but what instead works for you.

So choose what is actually the safest and best for you, not just what I'm outlining in this book.

Find a Mirror

With the mirror in front of you, choose how you would like to view yourself, either one specific body part (e.g., your stomach) or your whole body. If you are choosing to start with one specific part of your body, I would suggest covering the rest of the mirror with a cloth or, better yet, statements that can be encouraging for you in this process! I've had clients who have kept their mirrors covered throughout their work by putting inspirational or encouraging notes all around them. That's something that you can do to ease yourself into the activity and create safety.

Look at Your Body and Find Non-Judgmental Words

Alright, back at it. Take anywhere from 30 seconds to 1 minute to look at your body part; for our example, we are beginning with our stomach. Describe it in detail using neutral language. Note: What we are **not** doing here is using judgmental language. This is all about creating radical acceptance and building it. Examples of judgmental language are using words that embody a level of shame to them. Instead, we are using descriptive language that is neutral. Describe the freckles, the wrinkles, the stretch marks, the curves and so forth. These are descriptors, not judgments. Take away the shame that we've assigned to these body parts, the shame that we have intensified by adding meaning to these body parts.

Find Neutrality and Repeat Key Mantras

Sit for as long as you are able. Remind yourself that the body part embodies the neutral language you are using, not the critical judgment that you have heaped on it in the past. Create a mantra out of this language: my stomach has freckles, my stomach has a curve and my skin is peach colored. It's staying in this neutrality and stepping away from the negative language that creates the shift. Carry that neutrality with you throughout your day. When you fixate on something negative about your stomach, pull back up the neutral script as a counteract. It will not fix the negative feeling in the moment, but over time it develops a new language for your body.

Repeat the Practice

Practice this with each body part, building up little by little to the point that you have a neutral language with your body as a whole. As I said earlier, it's best to build up with the body parts that are easiest and most approachable at first—gain confidence and a renewed neutral belief system for yourself and then tackle the harder parts later. This can also be done with your body as a whole, and I recommend finishing out non-judgmental mirror exposure work with this activity. Build from the easiest up to the full body. It's a progression in exposure.

To tackle a full body non-judgmental mirror exposure, the best tactic is to dress in an outfit that leaves open some of the areas of your body that have historically been difficult for you. Engage in the same steps that we outlined above; utilize neutral language to describe each body part—no judgments, no shame. My body is tall, peach skin, wrinkles on my face, mole on my left cheek, hips that have curves, a curve in my spine, stretch marks on my stomach and back and so forth.

As I'm writing descriptors of my own body, what you might be thinking is that there are some "negatives" about some of these descriptors. But here's the very important thing: Stretch marks aren't negative, wrinkles are not either. The only reasons we have a negative association with these body attributes is because of a patriarchal society that has assigned value to what a body should look like. You can see these specific neutral statements as just that—neutral! This is why it has been so important for us to do the beginning work with understanding diet culture.

My Personal Experience with This Tool

And just so you are aware, I've practiced this myself in years past. When I was first working on recovery, there was a time when looking in the mirror sent me into a panic. I would feel angry and upset and frustrated with what I couldn't change. It was through radical acceptance, particularly non-judgmental mirror work, that I first took steps to care for my body and myself.

I remember the first time I attempted to view my body neutrally. I started with my stomach, and my initial thoughts were negative and critical "too big, poochy, misshapen." I had to pause, intentionally move those thoughts to the side and restart. Neutral language and neutral descriptors replaced the negative thoughts. My stomach has a mole, my stomach has curves, my stomach is peach colored and so forth. The more I practiced, the easier it became to shift to the neutral and away from the negative.

Slowly Shifting to Neutrality

This is an exposure of sorts. So many times, when people are working on poor body image, they simply avoid looking at their body. They cover up all the parts that they dislike. I've been there and done that myself in the past. It works in the moment, but it pushes the problem down the line. Instead of addressing the negative feeling you are having, you avoid and pretend you're not feeling it. Radical acceptance, through the tool of non-judgmental mirror work, focuses on body parts in manageable ways. What we're doing is so many things at once—tolerating viewing your body in small increments, shifting your language little by little from negative to neutral and then rewiring brain pathways to be able to tolerate more and more.

Here's an example: If I was afraid of snakes and I wanted to work through that fear, I wouldn't just avoid the snake. I would have to, little by little, adjust myself to the idea of the snake and then be able to get closer and closer to it and disentangle my fears from it. I would learn to tolerate it, moving toward radically accepting it. That's the key. The parallels are clear with radical acceptance of our bodies.

I know so many women specifically who avoid swimsuits and avoid shorts out of fear of having to see their legs or their stomachs or other trigger areas. And I understand why avoidance is necessary in the beginning. But we can't leave ourselves there. If we leave ourselves in avoidance, we don't give ourselves the opportunities to tolerate and then actually *accept* our bodies.

If we leave ourselves in avoidance, we don't give ourselves the opportunities to tolerate and then actually accept our bodies.

For example, if your thighs are a trigger point, you don't have to throw on a thong bathing suit bottom and just pretend you feel fine. That's like holding a snake when you're deathly afraid—it's impossible! But we use non-judgmental mirror work, we use slow exposures where we neutrally describe our thighs. We may be able to build up to wearing loose, long shorts in the beginning and describe our thighs with non-judgmental neutral language. As we progress, we may be able to wear shorter shorts and give ourselves grace and compassion during those times. It's all about shifting the work from avoidance to tolerance. Eventually, we land at the place of being able to wear what feels most comfortable and to be able to describe our body neutrally.

Spotlight Story

Candace was a client in her 30s. She and I had been working together for numerous years. Most of the work involved regulating eating patterns and poking holes in society's lies about what bodies, specifically female bodies, "should" look like. Candace had made so much movement in terms of caring for her body.

However, in our last year together, it became more and more apparent that one of the major ways Candace was tolerating the physical components of her recovery was to avoid and distract from body image. We discussed and understood this together in our therapy sessions, and we began to explore ways to start working on tolerating and accepting her body. One major component of this was to practice non-judgmental mirror work.

Prior to this, Candace had covered mirrors or specifically avoided looking into them as a means of tolerating her body. To work on radical acceptance, we began by spending only a few minutes looking in the mirror and with most of her body covered except for one of the easiest areas for her to tolerate. We described in neutral terms what this body part looked like—"I see my hands, the right one has a freckle, the nails are long and painted" and so forth. We reviewed the body part and went over and over it until the distress decreased, and then we moved on. From hands to arms, to chest, to stomach. The work was at times incredibly hard to tolerate, but Candace took it at her own pace creating safety and compassion for herself and her body throughout the process.

After a year of working on tolerating the components, she was able to take in her full body. We worked on describing neutrally each of her body parts, seeing and noting how she could shift the language she used to describe her body from critical to neutral. Although this one type of exercise did not completely shift Candace's experience of her body, it did open space for body neutrality. It did open space for her to begin connection versus avoidance of her body image. The work continued, and Candace was able to look in mirrors and begin enjoying parts of her body. It started with seconds and minutes of tolerating her hands and ended with being able to wear a swimsuit out at the local pool and tolerate seeing her reflection in the mirror.

Radical acceptance is hard; it is a complete shift from what we've been conditioned to believe about our bodies through diet culture and the diet industry's messaging. It flies in direct opposition to the idea that in order to accept our bodies, we have to change them. I know it is hard to believe this initially but think about it this way— you've tried the route of changing your body in order to accept it, and it has never been good enough.

Why not try accepting your body first free of any stipulations or criteria?

Why not try accepting your body first free of any stipulations or criteria?

Journal Topics

1   Does anything specifically scare you when it comes to non-judgmental mirror work? How might you be able to practice extra compassion with yourself for those particularly hard parts?
2   Are there areas of your body that are easier to radically accept? Are there specific areas that are more difficult?
3   Are there ways that you learned to avoid versus tolerate or accept your body throughout the years?

Only Have a Few Minutes? A Few Key Points to Focus On

1   Radical acceptance is a dialectical behavioral therapy concept we can utilize to help us manage negative emotions around our bodies. From this concept we find our next mantra for working through poor body image: *I can radically accept my body as it is*. In the concept of radical acceptance, we are radically accepting things as they are and not fighting against them.
2   We can grow in radical acceptance by our third tactic of *non-judgmental mirror work*. In this tactic we slowly radically accept specific parts of our body through a lens of compassion and neutrality.
3   We cannot avoid triggers (i.e., certain types of clothing and mirrors) in an effort to manage negative body image. The avoidance only takes us so far. Instead, conducting compassionate exposures with acceptance is a key component to changing our relationship with our body.

References

Cuncic, A. (2022, November 3). *How to embrace radical acceptance.* Very-well Mind. https://www.verywellmind.com/what-is-radical-acceptance-5120614

Griffen, T. C., Naumann, E., & Hildebrandt, T. (2018). Mirror exposure therapy for body image disturbances and eating disorders: A review. *Clinical Psychology Review, 65,* 163–174. https://doi.org/10.1016/j.cpr.2018.08.006

Linehan, M. (2022). *Building a life worth living: A memoir.* Random House.

Chapter 10

Moving to Love

Myth Debunked

"I might be able to appreciate a few parts of myself, but there will always be those last few things that I've just have to settle with hating."

We do not have to settle for hatred with parts of our bodies. Think about yourself as a small child, does that child deserve to feel "blech" about their stomachs or their thighs or that one "trouble area" that they just can't change?

We are conditioned to think this way about our inability to accept all our parts of our body from a society who makes money from our discontent. The concept of "fat talk" comes to mind with this. Fat talk is the conditioning of us, specifically as women, to make disparaging comments about our bodies or our food/exercise habits when in conversation with others. It's all too common, normalized and even encouraged among peers. And it sets the stage for us to believe that we should settle with negativity about parts of our bodies.

There is no need to stay stuck here. It is possible to care for, connect to and come to a place of compassion with ourselves and our bodies.

For this chapter, I wanted to start with a quote by Sonya Renee Taylor (2021), author, activist and game-changer in the world of self-love and body acceptance:

DOI: 10.4324/9781032654799-13

By refusing to accept body shame as some natural consequence of being in a body, we can stop apologizing for our bodies and erase the distance between ourselves and radical self-love.

(p. 12)

Read that quote again and sit with it for a second. Self-acceptance has a place, as does body neutrality—but they are just the beginning of the process. We can move beyond a neutral place to find actual radical self-love for who we are and what our bodies embody. We can move beyond neutral thinking to self-love.

Let's pause and think about the structure of this book so far. The first few chapters have discussed a general understanding for how we developed a poor relationship with our bodies—the historical roots of body hatred, the structures that are held up with our discontent. This is an important first step because we are establishing cracks in the wall; we are creating a deeper understanding for WHY we are so discontent with our bodies. We are learning to believe that it's not as simple as "our bodies are wrong" but more connected to a deeply ingrained societal belief system that creates discontentment to fuel a whole industry. It's important that we first understand the faulty logic before we can change our own beliefs. We're looking at the societal and familial structures that impact our body image.

We then moved ahead and outlined ways to first shift our thought structures around body image and body belief systems, our own mental health components that impact our body image. This is our second important step because thoughts affect feelings. What we think about our body becomes what we feel about our body. And what we feel about our body becomes our subjective truth. Remember, we're not fooling ourselves when we change or shift our thoughts, but what we're doing is pulling out the negativity that we have internalized from society's messaging and giving our bodies the chance to fight back. We're shifting our thoughts to make a difference in what we experience with our own bodies.

It makes sense then that the natural next shift we've taken in this journey is within the image that we see—what we physically see when we look in the mirror. It's so important for us to pause and understand that what we see is not necessarily true or accurate to reality. We are heaping all kinds of distorted messages and negative experiences onto our bodies' images.

And here's where our concept of radical acceptance and non-judgmental mirror work has come into play. What we are doing with this is not only shifting the lens through which we see ourselves but also shifting our ability to tolerate the difficult and uncomfortable emotions that can come with facing bad body image feelings. I can't stress enough the importance of this step—tolerating the discomfort.

So much of negative body image beliefs are built around the idea that the negative feelings we have about our body cannot be tolerated and must therefore be impulsively changed. But that route doesn't work. It can't work because the system is set up to fail. We can't shift our bodies and change our bodies and then find contentment with them. The fact that we feel that we have to change our bodies to find contentment with our bodies is inherently the problem. It's the opposite of contentment—it's discontentment to find contentment. This is why we learn to tolerate the distress and focus on radical acceptance to shift our perspective of what we see in the mirror.

Writing these initial steps out may make it seem like they are quick and easy—I assure you that they are not. It took me years to really come to terms with the lies I had internalized from the diet industry and the harm that my own negative thoughts had inflicted onto my body. I could barely do one of the mirror reflections at first. But little bit by little bit and by consistent repetition, I began moving away from entrenchment with negativity and into a realm of tolerance and acceptance with my body. You can too. We're deconstructing our ideas about our body and reconstructing a new belief system.

Finding Love for Our Bodies

What comes next in our journey is finding love for our bodies. What does it mean to love our bodies? There's a goal we have there that we haven't ever been able to attain, almost like an esoteric idea of where we are headed without a clear roadmap. Sometimes it can feel like trying to find the Great and Powerful Oz without a yellow brick road to lead the way.

What does it look like to love your body in terms of emotion and behavior? Some people who I've talked to don't like the idea of body love. They feel that it implies too much pressure and unrealistic ideals. "Surely you don't think we can actually *love* all of our body?"

Here's how I'll answer that question. I want to throw another word in here, one that I've been using a lot more recently as a synonym for body love: body respect. I often find that latching on to that terminology feels a lot more attainable. Body love can feel like a leap from body neutrality. Body respect can be the bridge that helps us get there.

Body love can feel like a leap from body neutrality. Body respect can be the bridge that helps us get there.

And here we are at our next mantra: *Body respect moves us to body love.*

Shifting to Body Respect

What do I mean by the language of body respect?

- To show someone or something respect means that we show a level of honor or deference to their needs.
- To respect means that we display compassion for their desires.
- To respect means that we treat someone or something in a way that trusts them.

To respect our bodies is just the same thing—it's to show compassion, trust and honor for all parts.

A Personal Experience with Body Respect

Early on in my recovery journey, I was plagued with feelings of hopelessness and low self-worth. I felt very certain that I would not and could not ever love the body I was in. I was stuck.

I remember one night when my self-loathing thoughts were incredibly strong—I was telling my college friend all the things I hated. She stopped me mid-sentence: "Johanna, stop. Try to tell me just one thing you like. Just one thing you can tolerate." I paused, it was a big shift for me to think this way. It took minutes of deliberation, but I finally settled on my feet.

She asked, "What would change if you focused on love for your feet every time you hated yourself?" This was a really funny thing,

I thought, and I was sure it would never change my self-hatred for the rest of my body. How does liking my feet shift my feelings about my thighs? But later that night I thought through what my friend was saying a bit more. It was then that I started thinking about a shift from just liking my feet to respecting my feet. If I respected my feet, I would show them gratitude for what they did. If I respected my feet, I would honor and care for them.

This shift catapulted me into a series of changes—if I shifted from negativity to respect for my feet, I could shift respect for so many parts of myself. Respect laid a foundation for trust, for honor and for compassion. What would it look like to be respectful to my feet, to my hands and to my other body parts?

Shifting to respect means that I don't have to believe every part of me is perfect; that's an impossibility and doesn't even make sense. What is perfect anyway? We've already established that our bodies will not ever live up to unrealistic standards that have been established. This idea of a "perfect" body comes from an industry that has built unrealistic standards. But body respect flies in the face of all of this: respect means that we honor the differences in our body and care for them. Respect means that we view our bodies from a lens of "What is good about this?" instead of "What needs to be changed about this?"

Respect means that we view our bodies from a lens of "What is good about this?" instead of "What needs to be changed about this?"

Tool 4: Respect for Each Part

And here we are at the next tool to use to shift your own relationship with your body. We call this tool *respect for each part*. With our past tools outlined in this book, each of the steps was very specifically outlined. With this tool, the task at hand is a little different. It's less structured and more of a mindful shift we make, little by little, body part by body part.

The beginning step is to choose a body part, perhaps the same one you started your mirror work with. As was the case with mirror work, I suggest starting with the most approachable of body parts. The one that you feel the safest with at the moment. And if you've started with the steps of mirror exposure work, the hope should be to have established an initial level of comfortability with certain parts of your body. Note: What I am not saying is complete comfortability! Each of these tools and skills builds one upon the other. And not one tool will help you achieve body acceptance, but put together and repeated over time, they help us move the needle closer and closer.

For this tool, you will need a hierarchical list of what are the most approachable body parts, and then the next and the next until you reach one of the hardest trigger points. This can be the same list that we've used in the past for non-judgmental mirror exposure work, or you can create a new list if things have shifted.

Give Yourself Time and Space If Needed

I know this is no small task to do, and even the act of it holds a high level of emotional intensity to it. Just a reminder, it is OK to start and stop parts of this book as needed. You are in charge of your body and can control how much you focus on these things at a time. You know yourself best.

If any tool that we are discussing becomes too arduous, it is OK to press pause for a time and return later. Similarly, it is also OK to skip certain parts and read on beyond them. Exercising autonomy over yourself is key for the process. Isn't that what we're working toward? Building respect and understanding for our body's needs, wants and boundaries?

Work on One Area of Your Body at a Time

Back to the tool at hand. Once you have established your working list of body parts—most approachable to most triggering—take your first body part and write it at the top of a piece of paper. For the example here, I am going to use the stomach. Underneath "stomach" written out, I created two columns. The first column says "Disrespect" and the other column says "Respect." You should create this worksheet using your own identified body parts.

Stomach

Disrespect   ////   Respect

This next step may be easy to do in recognition but difficult in terms of seeing the words stacked up on paper. I do think it's helpful, however, to see these words laid out. Without the acknowledgment of what shame has been heaped on a body part, it remains possible to keep it locked inside. It's in the releasing of the shame that we let go of the self-hatred. It's similar to releasing those shame-filled memories like we did in Chapter 5.

Under the disrespect column, write each of the things we know that we think and do (so both cognition and behavior) that contribute to disrespecting our specific body part. In this example, I am using a stomach. If I was doing this activity in some of my deepest body-hatred days, I would write down "name calling," "covering and hiding due to embarrassment" and "undernourishment and binging."

There are different ways a list like this may cause you to feel. Whatever emotions pop up for you are valid, be it feeling that your body deserves the negativity and disrespect or feeling hurt and being ashamed for treating your body this way. Oftentimes, clients will tell me that they feel both things at the same time, which makes a lot of sense given how stuck it can feel to be in endless cycles of body hatred. Whatever you feel in this process is OK. Let yourself feel it.

Here starts the part of the tool that can feel like a jump or a leap and may be a bit uncomfortable at first. But so much about working on body image issues is about sitting through and working through uncomfortable places, so please stick with this.

Let's turn our eyes to the respect portion:

• What kinds of thoughts and feelings and behaviors would you have if you engaged from a respectful standpoint with that body part?

It may be hard to think of body respect toward a place on your body where you feel shame. If this is the case, try to externalize it.

• What does it look like for someone else to respect their stomach?
• What does it look like for your partner or your child to respect their body?

Using an example of someone else does help to relieve the brick of shame that surrounds us in our wall. Again, if you are blocked for respect for yourself, externalize and think about someone who could show respect.

So let's put it back into action—go back to the example from above—the body part of the stomach. If I was to engage with my stomach from a place of respect, how would that look? What words would I list for that from the perspective of thoughts, behaviors and feelings?

To engage with my stomach from a respectful place, I would list words such as "nourishment," "kind words," "wearing clothes that allow my stomach to be seen," "listening to the hunger cues it gives" and "using lotions and creams to care for it."

Compare these two lists—there is such a stark contrast between the two sides. To show respect really shifts how you engage with this body part. Again, it's in direct opposition to the negative.

I understand that it's likely if you are reading this book you do not feel a level of respect for your body or certain body parts. What I'm not asking you to do is fake respect, but what I am asking you to contemplate is how it would be to engage drastically differently and in turn feel drastically differently in your body.

Your Body Has Done Nothing Wrong

You might be thinking, "But my body doesn't deserve respect," or a different version of how your body is failing you. This is why previous chapters were so important. We need to continue to understand that your body has done nothing wrong.

We need to continue to understand that your body has done nothing wrong.

Your body is functioning for you to the best of its ability. The problem lies in a society that has constantly told you that your body needs to be changed. If we see the lies with this, then we can understand in a deeper way why treating our body with respect is so integral and so deserved.

Two Things Can Be True at Once

I want to return to our discussion regarding bodies with chronic conditions or illnesses. In the face of a chronic, debilitating condition, phrases like "Your body is functioning for you at the best of its ability" can be off-putting. I understand it can feel as if your body is rebelling on you at times. It can feel as if there is an inability for your body to be valued in our society based on how it does or does not function by capitalistic standards.

I encourage you to hold two things at the same time, another nod to dialectical behavioral therapy and Marsha Linehan's (2014) skill work. Holding two opposing things at the same time is called a dialectic. Linehan (2014) says: "Dialectics allows opposites to coexist: you can be weak and you can be strong, you can be happy and you can be sad. In a dialectical worldview, everything is in a constant state of change."

Key Term:

Dialectic: Two opposing truths being true at the same time (Linehan, 2014).

Body Image and Chronic Conditions

In this world with body image and chronic conditions, it can be very difficult when people say, "Respect all the things your body does for you," when the reality is that you see and feel your body faltering in so many ways. I get it; it can feel trite and honestly downright impossible to feel connected to or respectful of a body when you are struggling physically.

A study conducted in 2018 on the U.S. population indicated that 51.8% of the total population was diagnosed with at least one chronic condition. "Prevalence was higher among women (28.4%) than men (25.9%) and increased with advancing age" (Boersma et al., 2020). And this study was limited to only 12 specific chronic conditions; the numbers increase as we account for and include more involved conditions, specifically those such as fibromyalgia or POTS, which have been increasing in diagnosis over these last several years.

The reality is that more and more people, specifically women, are struggling with chronic, debilitating conditions. To leave out this in a discussion on body image and body connection is to leave out a major part of the story.

Just because we are experiencing specific loss with our bodies doesn't mean that we can't find places of respect amidst that. The work is holding two opposing things at the same time: You can feel the loss and sadness AND you can find places to connect and respect your body. The two can exist together.

It is difficult to validate both at the same time, I know. And honestly, there are days when you just can't validate both at the same time. There are days when maybe the pain is too hard, or the fatigue wears you down. In the final chapters, we will discuss in-depth the reality of these types of days in body image recovery.

It's understandable that some days you can't connect as well to your body. It's OK if there are days when you don't feel as secure in your body. It doesn't mean that you aren't going to move forward in body image connection. In fact, having days of feeling off or discouraged with your body is a natural part of body image. This is especially true when you are struggling with a chronic condition.

In a chronic condition, we have days when we can feel connected and in tune with our physical needs. And we have days where we're barely able to make it through the day and managing a minute task can feel impossible. We can hold both things at the same time— there is so much loss to this. We get to feel and think and struggle with our bodies while also observing and holding on to respect for what they have done for us. This is our dialectic. It's our radical acceptance: a practice to come to that is very freeing when we can grasp it.

Back to our task. Take five minutes of your time every day to read your list. What you're working to do is shift your thoughts surrounding a particular part of your body. Again, simply reading a list doesn't make you love your body, but it's a step in the direction of showing care and compassion.

Engaging in Opposite Actions to Change Thinking

In DBT, we have a word for this type of work—opposite action. In her book, *Building a Life Worth Living: A Memoir*, Marsha Linehan (2022) writes: "Change your behavior and you will change your emotions" (p. 146).

There are many facets to this very short statement. One of the basic ways to think about it is directly related to opposite action. Opposite action is a "skill that involves choosing to do exactly the opposite of what your emotions tell you to do. When you think about it, we all have emotions that can cause us to make choices we'd rather not make" (Lorandini, 2024).

Let's break this down a bit:

- Do you feel anger at your body? When you engage with anger toward your body, what you will internalize is shame and even more anger with your body. Opposite action stands in, well, opposition to this.
- Do you feel anger toward your body but then you engage with it from a place of respect? That's an opposite action. And that in turn will shift your beliefs about yourself.

Key Term:

Opposite action: *A DBT skill that involves choosing to do exactly the opposite of what your emotions tell you to do.*

Linehan (2014) discusses the fact that an opposite action approach is only beneficial for changing emotions when these emotions are not justified for our circumstances. For example, to experience fear when faced with an assault is protective and important. An opposite action to this fear—approaching and connecting to the assailant—will not decrease the fear. The fear is protective and justified.

But let's think about this from our examples related to body image, I can speak to this specifically with my back and scoliosis. My initial feelings in my earlier life were shame and embarrassment. The behaviors were to hide my back, to avoid having it seen in pictures and, to attempt to pretend it was different than it is to make it presentable to others around me. But opposite actions to this are to show my back, to let it be seen in pictures, and instead of attempting to hide it, to care for it with proper stretching and strengthening. As I have worked on these opposite actions, as I have let my back be seen and cared for my back, I have begun to actually *respect* my back more. I have begun to appreciate my back.

Body Respect Will Lead to Body Love

Body respect lays the foundation for body love. We begin with respect, and we continue to tear down brick by brick that wall of shame built in front of us about negative beliefs with our body. We use body respect to build a new wall in front of us. And this new wall is built with behaviors and examples where we show ourselves and our bodies' respect.

- We create memories where even when we've felt disgruntled or upset about our bodies, we've given care and compassion and respect to them.
- We build a new brick of showing respect to our body in the face of feeling hard things.
- We build new memories of seeing that we can show compassion and kindness to our bodies even when feeling uncomfortable.

Distress doesn't have to be our foundation. It's in the undoing of these shame walls and the rebuilding of respect that we end up finding ourselves in a position to love our bodies.

Continue to practice *respect for each part* daily; take it body part by body part until you have worked through your hierarchy list. What you will eventually find is that what felt like a forced behavior will eventually turn into a new way of believing yourself. What felt like an impossibility becomes a possibility. Your new wall will involve bricks built together to form respect, which will lead to care and compassion and love.

In our next chapter, we will talk a little more about what body love really looks like (it may not be as extreme as you think!).

Journal Topics

1   What fears hold you back from showing your body respect?
2   Where do you believe those fears have surfaced from?
3   What would it look like to be free from those fears?

Only Have a Few Minutes? A Few Key Points to Focus On

1   It is possible to move from a place of self-hatred to neutrality and then to body acceptance and body love.
2   We can utilize the language of body respect as a bridge to move toward body acceptance and body love.
3   Our third mantra related to this is: *Body respect moves us to body love.*

4   The tactic we can utilize for this involves finding *respect for each part of our body*. We engage in this kind of respect utilizing opposite action (a DBT skill that involves choosing to do exactly the opposite of what your emotions tell you to do) in order to treat our bodies with specific respect in the face of negativity.

References

Boersma, P., Black, L. I., & Ward, B. (2020). Prevalence of multiple chronic conditions among US adults, 2018. *Preventing Chronic Disease, 17.* E106–110. https://doi.org/10.5888/pcd17.200130

Linehan, M. (2014). *Opposite action: Changing emotions you want to change.* Dialectical Behavioral Therapy Skills Training Video.

Linehan, M. (2022). *Building a life worth living: A memoir.* Random House.

Lorandini, J. (2024, February 21). *Opposite action for overwhelming emotions: How to make it work for you.* Suffolk DBT. https://suffolkdbtjl.com/opposite-action/

Taylor, S. R. (2021). *The body is not an apology* (2nd ed.). Berrett-Koehler.

Chapter 11

It's OK If You Don't Feel Good All of the Time

Myth Debunked

"In order to heal my relationship with my body, I have to love every part."

Thinking about body love in this sort of extreme way sets us up to stay stuck in body hatred. This type of dichotomous thinking is a part of an endless cycle of standards so high we can never measure up. Let's put it this way—part of body hatred is wanting our legs/stomachs/thighs to measure up to unrealistic ideals. AND an unrealistic ideal of body acceptance is to have to love every part.

Let's throw out unrealistic ideals and work on accepting where we are. Even in the most body confident of individuals, there are days when we will feel uneasy about certain parts of our body. We're in a society that tells us that our bodies are bad, but that doesn't mean body hatred has to take over again.

We can learn to care for ourselves through these days and to accept the times we don't fully embrace ourselves. It's all about nonjudgmental thoughts and compassion. We don't have to love every part of our bodies to care for, respect and be in connection to our bodies.

When I talk about body love and body acceptance, most people end up telling me how that would be impossible for them because they could never have that all the time. It feels as if being happy with your body 100% of the time is the goal. Guess what? It's not. I know,

DOI: 10.4324/9781032654799-14

that sounds startling, considering the fact that you came to this book to find peace with your body. But here's the thing: It's just that sort of fixation on perfectionism that causes us to stay stuck in cycles of body hatred. What do I mean?

Healing Your Body Image Is Not All or Nothing

We've been so conditioned to believe that there is perfection to attain with our bodies to make us feel good—in most cases this perfection is about the size of our hips or our arms. The industry constantly says, "Make your arms this size and you'll feel content." The perfectionistic components run deep, so deep that it even impacts our understanding of body acceptance. We feel that we must also be perfectionistic in how we think about our body. We conflate perfectionism with the size of our bodies and perfectionism around our beliefs about our bodies, believing that all things must be perfect in order for them to be good.

When we shift away from these negative messages, we sometimes hold on to perfectionism around our own belief systems. We end up thinking that we need to love our bodies 100% to actually develop a positive body image.

What we need to establish in this chapter is that it's OK to not be OK all the time with your body. In fact, you can have a bad body image day even when you are fully at peace with your body. Even I, in full recovery from an eating disorder, have days when I am not in love with all aspects of my body.

Does this sound strange? Maybe. I get that it's a little confusing to hear it said like this. But the reality is that waiting for full love around your body keeps you trapped in waiting instead of making the movement toward acceptance. It's like hoping for a magic wand to *poof* just make us love ourselves. And when we don't have that daily, we end up feeling like a failure and succumbing to more shame and guilt. Then the cycle of body shame continues.

A Few Personal Examples

Take my dog, Max. He's one of the cutest, most fun and most energetic puppies around. I love that dog to the moon and back. And I appreciate all the cute and beautiful things about him. But there are days where I have a hard time with his energy; maybe sometimes it's even straight up annoying, like when I'm trying to go to bed early and Max keeps barking. Ugh. So sometimes I feel less than enthusiastic about him. Sometimes there are days when he gets on my nerves. Does that mean I love Max less? Does that mean that I don't want him around? Nope, not at all.

Just because Max is sometimes (maybe, often) frustrating does not mean his value has changed. It does not mean he is not as good as he used to be. It does not mean there's anything less lovable about him. Max can have an off day and still be just as lovable. The same is true for me.

I remember throughout my own body empowerment journey feeling stuck in the belief that I would never be able to feel fully confident in my body. I thought to myself, "So why try?" I remember thinking that there would always be a cloud hanging over me, my thighs would never be good enough, my stomach would never be flat enough and more. But, with time and work, I was able to overcome this.

Part of the switch was that I stopped believing there was even a "good enough." Instead, I realized that there was just my body, living, breathing and existing in the world. I had days when I didn't feel confident in my skin and days that felt amazing. Amid all of that, my body continued to exist and function and just be for me. So again, it's OK if you don't feel great all the time. Your body is still your body.

Let's flash forward to more recent examples in my life. Guess what? I've gained weight over the past few years. I don't know my weight; I don't care about the number. But I do know a few of my pants haven't fit in recent years and that I've gone up in sizes. I remember a time in my life where that would have sent me into a spiral, full-blown panic. Maybe you're there right now yourself. Maybe even this paragraph is sending you into some major panic attacks. If that's where you are, it's OK. I was there as well.

Now at this point in my journey, I am OK with weight gain. It doesn't hurt me; my body is still good. My overarching belief systems have changed because I know that it is possible to feel confident in my body. But that doesn't mean that every day, all day, I love all the parts of my body. There may be days that I am not fully ecstatic about all parts of my body, but that doesn't mean I don't embrace and accept my body. The shift is that I'm not working against my body anymore. I'm not trying to control it. I'm letting it be what it is going to be—larger thighs and all.

And here's a reminder: I can do this because I've done the other underlying work of shifting memories, beliefs and thoughts around my body. Remember how I was told I had thunder thighs as a child? I removed that brick in my wall and replaced it with the belief that my thighs are strong, powerful and work for me. Now when my thighs have gotten bigger, it doesn't send me into a panic. I can acknowledge the change and still believe they're powerful. It's an act of rebellion, but rebellion doesn't look like all sunshine and roses. It also involves complex feelings. And that's OK.

My overarching belief systems have changed because I know that it is possible to feel confident in my body. But that doesn't mean that every day, all day, I love all the parts of my body.

Moving Beyond Our Bodies for Self-Worth

But let's take the focus off our bodies for a moment. There's also another way to talk about this.

- What if we became so interested in all the other aspects about ourselves that what our body felt like or what it looked like didn't take center stage?
- What if we understood "bad" body image days as feelings held up by hierarchical structures from our diet industry and diet culture versus something being wrong with our bodies?
- What if we were able to understand our body as simply a body, not something to be dissected or picked apart?

That would mean that we could experience days where maybe we didn't feel head over heels happy with our body or body image, but we didn't get sidelined by it. You know why? Because we are more interested in who we are than what we look like.

There's a phrase that floats around the body image recovery circle, and it's powerful. Here we are at our next mantra for our body image recovery work: *My body is the least interesting thing about me.*

I've had some clients tell me that at first glance this phrase is a bit off-putting. How is this thing that I've spent my whole life fixating on the least interesting thing about me? It's difficult to see it in this way when the bulk of your thoughts and mind have centered around it as a capstone.

Your Body Is Only Part of Who You Are

One of my favorite quotes that outlines this is by Glennon Doyle, author, speaker and activist who has recently opened up about her own struggles with body image and an eating disorder. She writes, "Your body is not your art—it's your paintbrush. Whether your paintbrush is a tall paintbrush or a thin paintbrush or a stocky paintbrush or a scratched-up paintbrush is completely irrelevant" (Doyle, 2020).

Our bodies are our tools to move forward in our lives. They give us the ability to do all the things that we love and enjoy. Let's return to our wall analogy. In earlier chapters, we talked about brick by brick being laid before you and creating a wall of shame. If we think about all these memories as building together to create a negative interpretation of ourselves, we could stretch the analogy further and understand the cornerstone to be an over-fixation on our bodies as the main source of our self-esteem.

Since writing the blog post I quoted above, Doyle shifted some of her thoughts about our bodies being tools. Many other authors have also discussed how our bodies are only a component of the artwork as well. However, we don't want to only see our bodies as tools. We don't want to only look at our bodies pragmatically in terms of their functions (i.e., this is what your body *does* for you) but instead we want to become enamored and accepting in terms of what is good and beautiful about our bodies as well.

From my clinical experience, we need a perspective of both seeing our bodies as tools AND seeing our bodies in radical acceptance. Our bodies are not only our tools, they are also our masterpieces. Especially when we've struggled with severe body image issues, it's often too big a leap to move from self-hatred to seeing our body as our artwork. Just like body respect is a stepping stone in our movement forward, so is body appreciation for what it can accomplish. Seeing our body in a pragmatic sense, as our paint brush, helps us develop a greater connection and appreciation for it and move toward more love.

We need to see that our bodies are NOT the summation of who we are. We need to be able to see our accomplishments without a fixation on our bodies to build ourselves up. This is a key component of body image recovery. Without this appreciation of how our body functions for us, we can get stuck in an endless loop of feeling that we can't move forward unless we change our bodies.

It's a vicious cycle, one that can never actually be satisfied—we feel low about ourselves having had a low self-esteem based on negative experiences of our bodies. We determine that fixing our bodies will be the thing that shifts our self-esteem and heals the negative memories, but the game is stacked against us. The culture is fixated on making it be that our bodies are never "good enough" so that we keep buying into the next diet or the next Botox injection.

Tool 5: Building You Up

Here's where we turn our attention to the tool we call *building YOU up*. What we've been looking at with each of our other skills is a breaking down and rebuilding of your internalized memories and self-dialogue. For this skill, we are looking to build you up in all other areas of your life.

To go back to Doyle's (2020) discussion, we are looking at all the ways you have painted beautiful masterpieces in your life. Again, our basic understanding is that your body "is the least interesting thing about you," so let's think about what all those other interesting things are about you. Let's build ourselves up to a place where we don't fixate on our bodies to be the thing that saves us from our insecurities.

For this tool, we'll get a little deeper into the concept of self-esteem. Because again, as we've said earlier in this book, everything that we think about our body is at the surface of what we think about our whole selves. Our basic self-esteem is at the core of our beliefs about our body.

What Is Self-Esteem and How Do We Build It?

Self-esteem, at its most basic definition, is our beliefs about ourselves. It can be high or low and can also fluctuate throughout our life. Some have described it as self-respect. It is built and developed in time, with our earlier years having an enormous impact on our self-esteem.

Remember our wall analogy with brick by brick of memories and beliefs about ourselves being laid in front of us? Each of these bricks symbolizes opportunities to develop and believe something about yourself. If those bricks overly feature and emphasize negative beliefs about your body, the development of a negative body image is heightened. But if they feature strong feelings and memories that build us up, we have a stronger foundation of ourselves as a person deserving of confidence and an overall stronger more positive belief about ourselves. Just like we talked about taking down and rebuilding beliefs about our body, we can do the same for our whole selves.

Key Term:

Self-esteem: *At its most basic definition, it is our own beliefs about ourselves.*

When I use the term whole self, I'm referring to both your body and your mind. Early in reworking our belief systems about our body, we will often separate body and mind; we call this externalization. Externalization, initially, can be helpful in separating the shame from our belief system. It's important, however, as we dive deeper into our work to incorporate the mind and body again in order to create integration. We incorporate the two together so that we build a fully connected person. Our mind and our body are together. This is the concept of embodiment, an important component of positive body image. We create strong self-esteem in that incorporation.

Self-esteem is made up of two parts—internals and externals. Externals are activities we engage in that build up our belief system about ourselves. Internals are the belief systems that we hold about ourselves. The two interact and connect to each other to create how we think about ourselves. Our tip in building a strong body image is to create a strong belief about yourself; this is where self-esteem lives. You are more than a body; you have so many aspects to you that encompass numerous interesting things.

You are more than a body; you have so many aspects to you that encompass numerous interesting things.

Author and speaker Kristin Neff has written several books on the concept of self-compassion and building a strong sense of love and self. In her book *Self-Compassion: The Proven Power of Being Kind to Yourself*, she discusses at length the practices of self-compassion. As individuals, we each have our particular things that make us us. We each have our own uniqueness, our own interesting ways that we think and feel and approach life's tasks. Neff notes that life is about accepting and connecting to each of these unique qualities with self-compassion (Neff, 2024).

What does this mean, and how does it shift our self-esteem when we approach ourselves with a level of self-compassion? To answer this question, we're going to turn to this fifth tool: **building YOU up**. In this tool, we are learning more about all the different elements of what make you, you. We can't develop a strong relationship with our bodies without also having a strong relationship with our whole selves.

We can't develop a strong relationship with our bodies without also having a strong relationship with our whole selves.

The active work for this tool is simple, but the internalization of it is the harder and integral part. Our tool involves two parts—we're going to look back and **build YOU up** in the past and then flip and **build YOU up** in the present.

Building Up Your Past and Present Selves

The first part involves your grabbing a few (possibly three or four) pictures of yourself throughout your childhood and teenage years. If you've worked on body image previously, you might imagine that we're going to have you look at these images from a body perspective. This work has value, but we're going to discuss it a little differently here. We are looking at ourselves from all parts and in all time periods. What is helpful for us in building ourselves up holistically is to look less at our bodies and more at our person in general.

Line up the photos you have in front of you, and then pause and think about the words from Neff's quote above: "strengths, weaknesses, gifts, challenges, quirks and oddities." Notice that her language surrounding aspects of a person does not have value judgments to it—there's no shaming language, no critiques. It's so much more nurturing than that and not critical. It's the underlying realization that we don't have to be perfect to be of value. Even further, it is our imperfections (i.e., oddities and quirks!) that make us our unique self.

Looking at the pictures of yourself, think about the strengths, weaknesses, gifts, challenges, quirks and oddities that you would use to describe yourself. Write out a list; if you notice that you are using judgmental language about yourself, scratch it out and think about how you would shift this.

Here's an example from my own life. If I were lining up pictures of myself, at various ages through my younger years, physically I would see a blonde little girl on the surface. But if I stuck to just this surface-level description, based on physical characteristics, I would be missing most of what makes up who I am. What I also need to do is describe who I was as a person. The list may look something like this:

- Vibrant
- Talkative
- Social
- Fearless
- Determined

What do you notice about my list? One major component is that I haven't assigned value to my list. Yes, these are descriptors that my little (ambitious) self always had. But I didn't list them in the negative. Think about the opposing attributes to this (and if you relate to my list, you may have also thought these things about yourself).

- Overwhelming
- Bossy
- Too much
- Reckless
- Stubborn

Whew, that doesn't feel as good to read, does it? Again, your list will look different than mine because you are you and I am me! But do you see how easy it was to flip to the negative?

I imagine that you have lived in some of the negative aspects about your own attributes before; I know I have. It bears continually repeating myself, but I need to keep reminding you that we feel negative about certain attributes more than others because of our external conditioning. And it's possible to shift this. I also want us to start with our younger selves with this tool purposely. We can be very disparaging with our adult selves, but beginning with our younger selves helps us make an important shift.

We have to understand that our beliefs about ourselves don't have to be 100% true all the time to be true. Think back to our chapter on changing our thought systems. There is a distortion at play when we don't believe we can embody an attribute unless it is perfect—all or nothing thinking. Just because you are not ALL nice doesn't mean you are completely NOT nice. It doesn't work this way. We need to be able to give ourselves these attributes free of negative conditioning and understand that we don't have to be each of them 100% of the time to embody them.

We need to be able to give ourselves these attributes free of negative conditioning and understand that we don't have to be each of them 100% of the time to embody them.

Let's look at the list of personality attributes you made. Where are you using judgmental language with yourself? Shift it—your judgmental voice is not serving you. When we're viewing this with our childhood self, it's much easier to shift the judgmental thoughts. That younger version of you did not deserve negativity and critique. You are a quirky, unique individual filled with strengths and weaknesses. And it goes without saying (but I'll say it anyway!) that you now do not deserve that negativity either. To go back to our first mantra, this is why it *all starts with gentleness.*

Story Spotlight

Sophia has experienced low self-esteem and low self-worth for as long as she can remember. She came to therapy looking to work on issues related to a long-standing battle with Anorexia Nervosa. We began by working on issues related to food and body image, but quickly in our work together Sophia realized how affected she was by an overall low belief system of herself. When asked to list attributes about herself, unrelated to her body or body image, Sophia could find almost nothing positive to say about herself or her personality. In our work together, we began to unravel the intertwined history of her poor sense of self connected to her poor body image. Sophia was able to see how "fixing" her body was done to strengthen her beliefs about herself as a whole. She didn't need more restrictive behaviors or more fixation with a number on a scale, what she needed was to build her self-esteem so that she could truly appreciate herself.

Together, we worked through the Build YOU up tool. We outlined positive attributes that she could hold onto for herself. The work was very difficult in the beginning, and it was almost impossible to find any positive beliefs for herself. However, as we looked back at her as a child, she was able to access more compassion and connection for her younger self. "Kind, free spirited, jovial. . ." Sophia listed the attributes for her 7-year-old self. Throughout the difficult experiences in her body image recovery work, Sophia constantly held on to these personality attributes that she was able to see in her younger self. As she grew in owning these attributes for herself, she grew in a stronger admiration and care for herself. This admiration laid the groundwork for an even stronger connection to her body.

Applying Constructive Thoughts to Your Present

I want you to take your list of personality attributes and write them clearly out for yourself—again free of judgments and critiques. Put them in a place that you will be able to see and think about often. Repetition is important in this situation. We are not lying to ourselves when we do this, but what we are doing is changing the script that we listen to. We've spent the time working on redirecting the negative thoughts from judgment and critique about our bodies to neutrality and then acceptance. Now comes the work of moving beyond our bodies being the central focus of ourselves and our lives. Holding on to these attributes helps us instill a much more positive and complete picture of ourselves.

Let's go back to my discussion regarding weight gain. My thighs got bigger—so what?!?! When we've also done the work to build up our personal beliefs about ourselves as a whole, not just about our bodies, we don't hold our body shape and size in such high levels of fixation. We instead know our bodies can shift and change in time, and the core value of self remains the same.

We are our bodies, but yet we are more than our bodies. Holding these two things at the same time helps us to move beyond the toxic emphasis that has been placed on our bodies. Instead, we can see our value with all that our body is in all its changes throughout time.

It's not likely that we will feel completely enamored with our bodies, and that's OK! As we've discussed above, if you struggle with a chronic condition, you know this feeling very well. There are days when your body is fatigued or has extra pain. There are days when it is just plain hard. And even if you do not have a chronic condition, this can still be the case.

We are not perfect in our perception of our bodies. In fact, acknowledging imperfection in all ways is part of the healing and rebuilding of our body image. But we can find a consistent and healthy relationship with our body because we also know and acknowledge all the amazing attributes that make up who we are.

Journal Topics

1   Has the idea of needing to 100% love your body kept you from working on body acceptance? If yes, how has this concept held you back in your journey?
2   Do you find the phrase "Your body is the least interesting thing about you" easy to accept or off-putting? Is it easy for you to see your body as a paintbrush, or do you find yourself fighting this concept?
3   What would change in your relationship with your body if you felt confident about all the other parts of yourself?

Only Have a Few Minutes? A Few Key Points to Focus On

1 It is a normal part of a healthy body image to have days where you feel off or less than ecstatic about certain parts of your body. This is particularly true because of the negative and critical body culture we are in.
2 It's imperative that we have a strong foundation of self-esteem in ourselves in order to build upon. Our next mantra: *Our bodies are the least interesting things about us.*
3 *Building YOU up* is a tool we can utilize to create strong belief systems surrounding not only our bodies but our identity and belief in ourselves in general.

References

Doyle, G. (2020, February 12). Your body is not your masterpiece. *Momastery*. https://momastery.com/blog/2014/07/06/body-masterpiece/

Neff, K. (2024, April 10). *Exploring the meaning of self-compassion and its importance*. https://self-compassion.org/the-three-elements-of-self-compassion-2/

Chapter 12

Embodiment

What Does It Mean to Be at Peace with Your Body?

Myth Buster

"Even if I find peace with my body at this age/size, I will end up hating it again if it changes."

Part of the lie fed to us from the diet culture is that a changing body is a wrong body. We end up internalizing that even if we can accept and care for our body in our 30s, 40s or 50s, all bets are off once we start to age. Or that all bets are off once we gain weight.

We have learned through this book that we are making space for our bodies to be allowed to change. We are giving care, compassion and grace to our growing and aging bodies. To age is to live. And it's only a culture fixed on invalidation of the human body that denies that.

The end goal is to be in connection, in validation and in compassion for our bodies. The end goal is to be embodied within our body to the point that we allow and embrace these changes. It is possible for your body to change and for you to continue your compassionate care for it.

Seventy percent of girls with a poor view of their bodies won't be as vocal about their own opinions on issues and things (Dove, 2018). I've laid out some staggering data throughout this book, but when I came across this fact while researching, it stopped me in my tracks. We are raising a generation of young girls who are silencing themselves due to body image issues.

DOI: 10.4324/9781032654799-15

Reflect back on your own history. I imagine you might see a similar pattern. I can say the same for myself—little Johanna was boisterous, loud and a boss. But in my most body insecure state, I was not able to use my voice any longer. I was hesitant, I was timid. And I was disconnected from myself in all ways. I disconnected my mind from my body because of the deep insecurity. This is the disconnect that causes us pain. As I've said countless times throughout this book:

- We deserve to take up space.
- We deserve to be vocal about our thoughts, needs and opinions.
- We deserve to give confidence and voice to our beliefs and to ourselves.

Through this book we've been building up your confidence in your body, and my hope is that we are also able to build up a belief in your voice as well.

Through this book we've been building up your confidence in your body, and my hope is that we are also able to build up a belief in your voice as well.

Embracing Embodiment

Instead of disconnecting, instead of shrinking, your goal is to grow the mind and body back together. The ultimate goal is embodiment. This is a big buzz word that's been floating around the eating disorder recovery world a lot more recently. Although we are now starting to talk about embodiment in recovery spaces, many cultures have been engaging with life from an embodied perspective for centuries: Buddhist belief systems are centrally focused on embodiment, and Native American and Black cultures have historically preached about being one with your body.

This is only new to our Western white culture because we have spent years disconnecting our minds and our bodies—phrases like "Mind over matter" or "Push through the pain" come to mind when we think about this. Culturally speaking, so much of Western cultural practices have been about disconnecting ourselves from our bodies, rather than being at one with our bodies. This is particularly true for women in our culture who have been conditioned to engage in distrust of their bodies.

Key Term:

Embodiment: *The ability to feel a connection between mind and body* (Perey & Cook-Cottone, 2020).

The Prevalent Mistrust of Women's Bodies, Particularly for BIPOC Women

There's so much research on this. Black and Latinz women, especially, but white women too, are told that their pain and body experiences are invalid. A study conducted by the Centers for Disease Control and Prevention in 2021 indicated that non-Hispanic Black women were at a 2.6% higher rate of maternal mortality than non-Hispanic white women (Hoyert, 2023). Why? Numerous reasons, but story after story indicates that a major part is how Black women have been silenced about their experiences in their own bodies.

Icon, tennis star and activist Serena Williams experienced this after giving birth (Lockhart, 2018). She knew her body, she knew when it felt good and when it felt off. In her accounting of the event, she knew she had a history of a life-threatening embolism. She began experiencing shortness of breath following the birth of her daughter and alerted both the nurse and the doctor. Instead of responding with validation and action, the doctor and the nurse dismissed and offered different feedback about what was occurring. Williams knew what her body needed, she knew what was happening and she was told to discount it. This story highlights how Black and brown women are not listened to and how Black and brown women are told not to be IN their body but to distance themselves from their bodies' needs, even while their bodies are being exploited for others' gains.

Corrosive External Influences Shut Down Intuition

In little and big ways, all women are told not to believe their pain. They are told to silence their bodies and listen instead to outside influences. This interrupts our ability to hear our bodies, to listen to them. This interrupts our embodiment. I know too many women who have been conditioned to push past hunger, to restrict themselves, in order to lose those last 5, 10 and 15 pounds before a date, often Memorial Day.

The "beach body" phenomenon comes to mind. The origin of getting "bikini body ready" is from—you guessed it—the diet industry. It "was first popularized in a 1961 ad campaign by a chain of weight-loss salons called Slenderella International" (Robb, 2014). Silence your desires, silence your needs and silence your body all in the name of finding an obscure, unrealistic ideal for yourself. For years we've been obeying this lie. I hear it every spring in workout classes, at dinners and so forth. "How many days till Memorial Day, ladies?" What is being preached is a push to disconnect from our needs and silence our bodies.

Changing the Message

This is our final mantra: *I can be embodied, fully present and involved in my body.*

Embodiment is the opposite of the silence we held on to in our criticalness and judgment. In being embodied we are so involved and connected to our bodies that we let them guide us. We listen, we respond and we are our bodies. As stated before, we first work through our thoughts as we heal our body image. But full healing brings our mind and our bodies back together, connecting both in a way that creates not only a relationship but a togetherness.

A friend asked me recently about what shifts when we are able to find peace with our bodies. Her questions were as follows:

- What's the hope with shifting poor body image?
- Do we actually change how we feel about our bodies?
- Or do we change how we deal with what we feel about our bodies?

This distinction is so interesting. Can you really change how you *feel* or are you just changing what you *do*? My short answer is that you can do both! That's what this book has aimed to do— show you how to do both.

If we've lived with years of self-hatred and animosity with our bodies, we first must shift how we deal with how we feel about our bodies. This first shift involves:

- Reframing behaviors around food intake.
- Understanding why we feel as we do about our bodies based on the past.
- Changing our behaviors in how we view our bodies and what we do around self-reflection and mirrors.

This is what we do initially. *But* those first behavioral shifts begin to add up to a second, next level shift: This is where we shift what we feel about our bodies. The second shift involves the realization that we are in our bodies, we are no longer criticizing but are living in and being in. This is embodiment.

We are in our bodies, we are no longer criticizing but living in and being in. This is embodiment.

Identifying Empathy to Move Forward

Sonya Renee Taylor (2021), in her book *The Body Is Not an Apology*, has this to say: "When we liberate ourselves from the expectation that we must have all things figured out, we enter a sanctuary of empathy" (p. 22).

So much of being in our body is to challenge the expectations we've placed on it, to let go of the critiques we've made and find connection to it again. Empathy is a bridge to this.

Embodiment is all about empathy at its core. We can't BE IN our body without also having a level of compassion for it. If we don't feel the empathy and compassion for it, we are constantly at odds, fighting with it rather than living in it. In my own story, this looked like years of diets and exercise (in the name of an eating disorder) to fight against the natural weight my body wanted to be. There was nothing empathic in those patterns; it was all critique, judgment and self-hatred. And it left me feeling disconnected and angry with my body, not happy.

Looking at my thighs and all their changes over the years with empathy has created a shift for me. This change means I don't look into disconnection (i.e., diets and sculpting tools) to manage any off-putting days with my body; instead, I go deeper INTO my body. Going deeper into your body means that you let go of the outside culture's expectations of what it should be. You are not in opposition to it anymore, instead you are your body and it is you, no distinctions anymore.

Going deeper into your body means that you let go of the outside culture's expectations of what it should be.

I want to be careful here: Empathy does not denote some level of pity or sadness. In fact, when I have empathy and embodiment, I feel proud of my thighs and proud of my body. I move past neutrally into pride for myself and my body.

Key Term:

Empathy: *Being aware, compassionate and connected to the feelings and needs of others.*

Embodiment Takes Time

Embodiment is the focus of our last chapter for a specific reason. It can sound like it's just a simple step. "Just be in your body." It is not this simple if you've been living for years with self-hatred. Instead, embodiment is an involved process that requires many steps to undo messages and recreate the next steps beyond. It's deconstructing and rebuilding, just like we've been doing throughout this book.

Beyond just rebuilding, embodiment is reconnecting so that we can feel tangibly connected and close to our bodies again. It's a reconnecting so that our mind and body are once again together. It's a reconnecting so that while we are walking, running, gardening or doing whatever else with our bodies, we are simply IN our bodies, not scrutinizing or judging.

Oftentimes, I've noticed it can be difficult to give specific tools to be involved and connected to one's body. One thing that we've often had to do to cope with our body self-hatred is to disconnect, even disassociate, in order to cope with our body image issues. I did it myself. Years of teaching myself to disconnect from my body and now you tell me to be back in my body?! But how?! And why?! It never made sense to me in my deepest parts of self-hatred.

Remember my discussion of my initial motivators—my initial "ah-ha" moments? I was reading Anne Lamott's book *Traveling Mercies*. She was getting ready for the beach, putting on a bathing suit (something she avoided for years) and choosing to put lotion all over her thighs, calling them her "aunties." This was my lightbulb moment: I would say it moved me into the space of realizing that I could be in my body—embodiment per se—without judgment.

This aha moment didn't move to embodiment right away. I had years of work cut out for me, undertaking so many of the things that I wrote about earlier in this book. I did the work, I undid the thoughts and I changed the beliefs. I tolerated the clothes I had avoided for years.

In my own recovery work, I began by tolerating difficult feelings (Chapter 9), undoing negative messages (Chapter 8) and changing belief systems (Chapter 10), but it was months and years of repeating these changes that created the ultimate change for me.

Where I landed was embodiment. Where I landed was a place of connecting to my body as I hadn't before. You can land there as well. Back to our final mantra: **You can be embodied, fully present and involved in your body.**

Final Thoughts: Be Patient with Your Internal Work

I have a garden, and this spring I decided to plant a bunch of wildflowers in one part. Initially it was a little discouraging. I spent countless hours taking care of the seeds, watering and cultivating growth, and what it looked like I got was a bunch of weeds popping up. And really, I thought it was a bunch of weeds popping up! It seemed to me that my wildflowers had died and what I had cultivated was a bunch of weeds. And then just the other day, all of a sudden a bunch of beautiful flowers popped out of those weeds. You might get where my metaphor is going here—this work can be really exhausting. It can feel as if the tips, tools and hours that we're putting into changing our feelings about our bodies are to no avail. It might feel like all we're getting are a bunch of weeds.

Clinically speaking, so many times I've watched clients start the work and leave the work. It is difficult, it is exhausting and at some points it feels damn near impossible. I don't blame a single person who struggles to keep going. I get it completely. But my hope with this book is to encourage you to stick with it. You learned these behaviors, these thoughts and these core beliefs about your body. Getting stuck in negative beliefs has caused so much pain. It is possible to change your experiences with your body. Please don't give up.

It is possible to change your experiences with your body. Please don't give up.

For some time, the work might look like weeds, and you will question if it really is worth it and if all this work amounts to anything. It's like logging a lot of hours watering something with hopes that it will actually produce. It really might look like weeds initially or that you are not really going to make changes. Stick with it, the flowers come. It's not just weeds that you're growing.

We've come to the end of our journey, but that doesn't mean that the work is done. You will find you may need to repeat some of these steps or keep the tools close for some time to work on changing your behavior and thought patterns. That is OK! Reading this book once will not change your beliefs overnight. It will take repetition and changing your thought patterns over time.

I have changed my beliefs with my body; I've seen clients change their beliefs. It is possible. Finding peace with your body is available to you. Expect to be discouraged during the process. That is normal. There will be days of feeling like it is impossible. Stick with it. The flowers will come.

Journal Prompts

1   Is there anything that frightens you about the concept of embodiment? Anything that causes apprehension or misgivings?
2   Are you finding yourself in the "weeds" vs "flowers" section of your body image restoration journey? If yes, can you list a few places that you are starting to see the flowers pop up? Can you highlight any moments where you see yourself reconnecting to your body again?

3 What parts of the healing journey continue to be difficult for you? Is there a tool or mantra you can return to in order to continue your work? Outline and do that now.

Only Have a Few Minutes? A Few Key Points to Focus On

1 Embodiment is the ability to feel a connection between mind and body. The goal throughout all of our work has been to move from hatred to neutrality, to connection and finally to embodiment.
2 Embodiment means that we are in our bodies, fully present, that we no longer scrutinize or disconnect our minds and bodies from each other.
3 Women, specifically at even higher rates Black and brown women, have been taught to discount their emotions and invalidate their needs.
4 It is imperative that we believe our needs and validate our desires as a part embodiment.

References

Dove. (2018, June 29). New Dove research finds beauty pressures up, and women and girls calling for change. Retrieved November 16, 2020, from https://www.prnewswire.com/news-releases/new-dove-research-finds-beauty-pressures-up-and-women-and-girls-calling-for-change-583743391.html

Hoyert, D. L. (2023). Maternal mortality rates in the United States, 2021. https://www.cdc.gov/nchs/data/hestat/maternal-mortality/2021/maternal-mortality-rates-2021.htm#:~:text=In%202021%2C%20the%20maternal%20mortality,for%20White%20and%20Hispanic%20women

Lockhart, P. (2018, January 11). Serena Williams's health scare shows how medicine dismisses black women. *Vox.* https://www.vox.com/identities/2018/1/11/16879984/serena-williams-childbirth-scare-black-women

Perey, I., & Cook-Cottone, C. (2020). Eating disorders, embodiment, and yoga: A conceptual overview. *Eating Disorders*, 28(4), 315–329. https://doi.org/10.1080/10640266.2020.1771167

Robb, A. (2014, July 23). Why can't we stop talking about "ikini bodies"? *Slate Magazine.* https://slate.com/human-interest/2014/07/the-history-of-the-term-bikini-body-explained.html

Taylor, S. R. (2021). *The body is not an apology* (2nd ed.). Berrett.

Index

Note: *Italic* page numbers refer to figures.

For Product Safety Concerns and Information please contact our EU
representative GPSR@taylorandfrancis.com
Taylor & Francis Verlag GmbH, Kaufingerstraße 24, 80331 München, Germany

www.ingramcontent.com/pod-product-compliance
Lightning Source LLC
Chambersburg PA
CBHW071744270326
41928CB00013B/2792

9 781032 654775